TALENT:

STRATEGY, MANAGEMENT, MEASUREMENT

Carole Tansley

Paul Turner

Carley Foster

Lynette Harris

Anne Sempik

Jim Stewart

Hazel Williams

The Chartered Institute of Personnel and Development is the leading publisher of books and reports for personnel and training professionals, students, and all those concerned with the effective management and development of people at work.
For full details of all our titles, please contact the Publishing Department:
Tel: 020 8612 6204
E-mail: publish@cipd.co.uk

To view and purchase all CIPD titles:
www.cipd.co.uk/bookstore

For details of CIPD research projects:
www.cipd.co.uk/research

TALENT:
STRATEGY, MANAGEMENT, MEASUREMENT

Carole Tansley

Paul Turner

Carley Foster

Lynette Harris

Anne Sempik

Jim Stewart

Hazel Williams

NOTTINGHAM BUSINESS SCHOOL, NOTTINGHAM TRENT UNIVERSITY

First published 2007
Reprinted 2007, 2008, 2009

Cover and text design by Sutchinda Rangsi-Thompson
Typeset by Paperweight
Printed in Great Britain by Short Run Press, Exeter

British Library Cataloguing in Publication Data
A catalogue record for this book is available from the British Library

ISBN-13   978 1 84398 189 3

Chartered Institute of Personnel and Development,
151 The Broadway, London SW19 1JQ

Tel: 020 8612 6200
Website: www.cipd.co.uk

Incorporated by Royal Charter. Registered charity no. 1079797.

CONTENTS

LIST OF CASE STUDIES

LIST OF FIGURES AND TABLES

ACKNOWLEDGEMENTS

The CIPD would like to thank the researchers at Nottingham Business School and the case-study organisations that contributed to this research, including:

Cargill
Derby City Council
Google
Gordon Ramsay Holdings
Legal Services Commission
London and Quadrant Group
North West Wales NHS Trust
PricewaterhouseCoopers LLP
Standard Chartered PLC

We would also like to thank the following members of the project's steering group for their contributions:

Kim Birnie	Leap Ahead Ltd
Janice Caplan	Scala Associates
Jonathan Ferrar	IBM
Karen McKibbin	Harvey Nichols
Sue Newhall	
Dan Simpson	Siemens
Fran Spencer	
Michael Staunton	VT Group plc
Jennifer Taylor	Further Developments
Alan Warner	Hertfordshire County Council

FOREWORD

Talent management is increasingly seen as a critical success factor as organisations strive for competitive advantage. A new survey across 17 EU countries (by Boston Consulting Group and the European Association for Personnel Management) finds 'managing talent' is the most critical challenge facing HR.

And CEOs as well as HR directors are now likely to number talent management among their key priorities.

But what does talent management actually *mean*, and what is being done in organisations to manage talent?

The drivers for talent management seem reasonably clear, even if its specific meaning is less obvious. Persistent skills shortages, the changing demographics of the UK workforce, its increasing diversity and the work–life balance agenda have led to increased competition for individuals who are capable of making the greatest difference to organisational performance.

In the current tight labour market this has given rise to what has been labelled 'the war for talent'. The ability to attract and retain higher-quality individuals than competitor organisations is increasingly a strategic priority for business. How this is to be achieved is a growing preoccupation for chief executives and senior managers, and those responsible for the design and delivery of HR strategies that proactively support the needs of the business.

At the heart of this growing interest in talent management is a recognition that it is not enough just to attract individuals with high potential. There must be a planned strategy for managing their talents which is supported by processes to develop the investment in human capital, retain the commitment of talented employees and properly utilise their abilities.

In order to better understand the growing phenomenon of talent management the CIPD commissioned a team at Nottingham Business School to undertake further research in this area, to look at how organisations are identifying, developing, deploying and retaining talent, and to determine to what extent this is part of a proactive approach to talent management. The research draws primarily on face-to-face interviews within nine case-study organisations, allowing an in-depth exploration of what talent management means within different contexts and the different approaches used.

You may be just beginning to consider what talent management means for your business. Or you may be looking for opportunities to improve practices and embed ways of working. We hope this report provides you with some advice, suggestions and ideas on your talent management journey.

Rebecca Clake
Victoria Winkler
CIPD Research and policy

EXECUTIVE SUMMARY

This report presents findings from an in-depth study of talent management in nine organisations across a wide range of employment sectors. The study, commissioned by the CIPD, was prompted by the growing importance of effective talent management to organisational success. The aim of the study is to provide insights into the approaches being adopted by employers of different sizes and sectors as a guide to other organisations working on their own talent programmes. Although there was a wide variety of views about talent and how to manage it, there were also some common approaches through the case-study organisations. This report, *Talent. Strategy, Management, Measurement*, will present these practical examples.

Developing the potential of the workforce is becoming a priority issue in many organisations because of a variety of internal and external forces. Persistent skills shortages, the changing demographics of the UK workforce, its increasing diversity and the work–life balance agenda have led to a very tight labour market resulting in increased competition from organisations for individuals who are capable of making the greatest difference to performance. The result has been increased competition to attract and retain individuals who demonstrate the most potential. Social and legislative factors have created further challenges resulting in the need for new approaches to talent management on the part of HR professionals and their organisations. These approaches are likely to include both talent strategy and the execution of that strategy as well as talent acquisition, development, management and retention.

Furthermore, the value of having an effective, organisation-wide talent management process in place was evident. Our research found that such a process provided a focus for investment in human capital and placed the subject of talent high on the corporate agenda – a desirable objective for HR

professionals. It was in addition concluded that the focus on talent management also contributed to other strategic objectives, such as building a high-performance workplace or a learning organisation; adding value to the employer of choice and branding agenda; and contributing to diversity management. So an effective approach to talent management has many tangible benefits that cross over into other areas of the HR function.

As well as these conclusions, our research sought evidence of a consistent definition of 'talent' from the evidence across the nine case studies and from over 100 interviews. Although, not surprisingly, there were many views about the nature of talent, it was possible to distil these into a definition that can provide a working basis for the development of a talent management strategy:

> *Talent consists of those individuals who can make a difference to organisational performance, either through their immediate contribution or in the longer term by demonstrating the highest levels of potential.*

Similarly, research into the processes of talent management also led to a wide range of practices that tended to be organisation specific and dependent upon the context within which talent management was taking place. But once more a definition was derived from various examples of successful practice in this and other research projects as:

> *The systematic attraction, identification, development, engagement/retention and deployment of those individuals with high potential who are of particular value to an organisation.*
>
> *Talent Management: Understanding the dimensions,*
> CIPD Change Agenda, 2006

These two definitions arose out of the research and provided a language for further analysis.

The definition of talent and talent management and the perceived value of having a talent process in place were complemented by a range of valuable findings that will prove useful for those organisations looking to establish their own approaches to talent management – whatever terminology they use to describe it. These are outlined below:

✤ A successful approach is based on an agreed, organisation-wide *definition of talent and talent management*. Such definitions form the springboard from which both talent strategy and talent management processes can be launched.

✤ In addition, a *language for talent management activities* that is understood by all the parties in the employment relationship is a strong requirement.

✤ *A proactive, strategic approach to talent management* offers considerable organisational benefits in terms of developing a pool of talent as a resource to meet identified needs.

✤ *Support for talent management must flow from those at the very top of an organisation* and cascade throughout.

✤ *Engaging line managers from an early stage* is critical to ensure that they are committed to organisational approaches to talent management.

✤ *Talent management can be used to enhance an organisation's image and supports employer branding* in the labour market as well as a providing a means of enhancing employee engagement to improve retention.

✤ *Talent management activities should be developed with other HR policies and practices* for a joined-up approach.

✤ Developing talent may be based on *a blend of informal and formal methods*.

✤ *HR specialists have an important role to play* in providing support and guidance in the design and development of approaches to talent management that will fit the needs of the organisation.

✤ Processes must be developed to *track the performance and progress of those identified as talent*.

A final conclusion was that talent management was a dynamic process that has to be continuously reviewed to ensure that organisational requirements are still being met in the light of changing business priorities. Ultimately, organisational success is the most effective evaluation of talent management.

TALENT: STRATEGY, MANAGEMENT, MEASUREMENT

TALENT– A STRATEGIC PRIORITY

There is a war for talent.

Persistent skills shortages, the changing demographics of the UK workforce, its increasing diversity and the work–life balance agenda have led to a very tight labour market resulting in increased competition from organisations for individuals who are capable of making the greatest difference to performance.

A combination of these challenges has made the ability to attract and retain talented individuals a strategic priority for many organisations, and this is likely to be on the radar of the Chief Executive Officer and the board. There is growing pressure on HR professionals to deliver effective strategy, policy and programmes in support of this challenging objective.

Central to this growing interest in talent management is the recognition that it is not enough just to attract individuals with high potential. Developing, managing and retaining those individuals as part of a planned strategy for talent is of equal importance. Effective processes to measure the return on this investment in human capital have also been identified as part of the overall perspective of talent. These compelling factors led the CIPD to commission a year-long research project to look at how organisations are identifying, developing, deploying and retaining talent, and to what extent this is part of a proactive approach to talent management.

The initial focus of the research was to establish what factors were driving this increased focus on talent management. We found that a wide range of factors had converged into a powerful force for change. These factors are outlined in Figure 1 on page 2.

This combination of external factors as well as workforce demand and supply issues were identified in various degrees in our case-study organisations. Notwithstanding private/ public sector differences, the responses of our interviewees revealed a great deal of commonality in the factors they identified as impacting on their management of talent. These are summarised in the box on page 2 and are examined in more detail in the CIPD's recent Change Agenda *Talent Management: Understanding the dimensions* (CIPD, 2006).

Other issues prompting an interest in talent management in our case-study organisations include:

❖ employers having increasingly to accommodate the changing expectations and preferences of individual employees if they want to attract and retain the most talented individuals. In tight, highly competitive labour market conditions it is recognised that talented people, whose skills are in demand, are increasingly able to negotiate the employment package that most appeals to them.

❖ developing a reputation as an employer of choice and a concern for employer branding.

Figure 1 ❖ Demand, supply and context factors for talent management

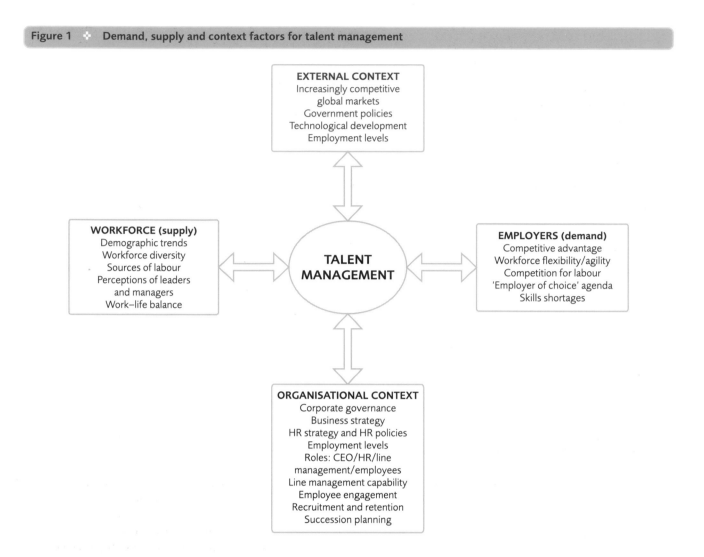

IDENTIFIED WORKFORCE CHALLENGES FOR TALENT MANAGEMENT

❖ Changes in the workforce due to an increasingly global labour market and greater workforce diversity.

❖ Alterations to the demographic trends in the UK. By the year 2020 it is projected that the UK workforce aged 20–40 will decrease by 16 million and those aged between 45 and 65 will increase by 17 million.

❖ Less loyalty to one employer from individuals who self-manage their careers and development. These people have greater access than ever before to information about career opportunities, legislative changes, such as alterations to the statutory retirement age, pensions, age discrimination legislation and provisions for working parents and carers.

❖ More flexible ways of working combined with a growth in the virtual workplace and the growing priority given by individuals to work–life balance.

❖ A shift in emphasis to the quality of contribution made while at work, rather than the hours spent at work (Bonney, 2005; Kersley *et al*, 2006).

❖ A continuing growth in the numbers of women in the workforce and issues of their representation in senior roles.

❖ More people working part-time and the associated challenge of making the most of the talents of individuals not working in full-time roles.

Table 1 ❖ The main objectives of talent management	
Main objectives	% of respondents
Developing high-potential individuals	67
Growing future senior managers	62
Enabling the achievement of strategic goals	42
Meeting future skills requirements	38
Attracting and recruiting key staff	36
Retaining key staff	33
Supporting changes	17
Addressing skills shortages	16
Assisting organisational resource planning	13
Redeployment of staff to other roles	12
Other	2

Source: CIPD Learning and Development Survey (2006)

The CIPD 2006 Learning and Development survey gave further evidence of this focus by revealing the most common reasons for investing in talent management activities. These are: developing high-potential individuals, growing future senior managers, and enabling the achievement of strategic goals.

The priority given to the different drivers is set out in Table 1

In the majority of our case-study organisations the prime reason for investing in talent management is to develop individuals identified as having high potential for the future, bearing in mind the sector and the nature of the work. But there was also a need to meet today's business demands for talented individuals to maintain competitive advantage.

In summary, our research demonstrated that the forces driving the increased interest in talent were a potent mix of external supply issues and internal organisational demands.

TALENT MANAGEMENT RESEARCH

To provide further detailed evidence, the report draws on two types of information; first, a series of in-depth case studies involving the nine organisations listed in Table 2 gives a hands-on account of the reality of talent management as it is put into practice. The richness of the information produced is complemented by, second, a wide range of sources that had already contributed to an understanding of talent management, including the CIPD publications:

❖ two Change Agendas – *Talent Management: Understanding the Dimensions* and *Reflections on Talent*

Management (available at www.cipd.co.uk/changeagendas)

❖ the 2006 Learning and Development annual survey (available at www.cipd.co.uk/surveys)

❖ reports and surveys on learning and development; recruitment, retention and turnover; flexible working; diversity and international issues.

The case studies (outlined in Table 2 on page 4) complemented this information by raising a number of issues:

❖ how talent is defined in different organisational contexts

❖ the drivers for talent management initiatives

❖ different approaches to talent management

❖ issues and challenges faced by organisations in talent management

❖ the extent to which talent management is linked to overall business strategy

❖ links between talent management and other HR policies and practices

❖ evaluating the success of talent management interventions.

A combination of published research and new information from the case studies is the basis of the insights about talent management included in this report.

Case study	Type of organisation	Number of employees
Cargill	Global provider of food, agricultural and risk management products and services. It is one of the world's largest companies with annual sales of approximately $75 billion.	c149,000
Derby City Council	A local authority providing all government services for the 237,000 people who live in Derby city.	c12,000
Google	Google.com is one of the five most popular sites on the Internet and is used around the world by millions of people. It is the world's largest search engine.	c5,000
Gordon Ramsay Holdings	The organisation has a London head office, nine leading restaurants in London, consultancies in Dubai and Tokyo, and media and consultancy interests.	c900
Legal Services Commission	LSC is an executive non-departmental public body which maintains and develops the Community Legal Service and Criminal Defence Service.	c1,700
London and Quadrant Group	The Group is a not-for-profit organisation whose main objective is to offer high-quality affordable housing to people in Greater London and the south-east of England.	c800
North West Wales NHS Trust	The Trust serves a population of c240,000 and transient/seasonal workers and holidaymakers in the summer months.	c5,500
Pricewaterhouse-Coopers LLP	The organisation operates in 149 countries providing solutions for businesses and the capital markets.	c140,000
Standard Chartered PLC	The bank has an extensive global network of over 1,400 branches representing over 100 nationalities worldwide.	c60,000

Table 2 ❖ **The talent management case studies**

RESEARCH METHODOLOGY

The main focus of the study is a number of organisations representing a wide range of sectors which included manufacturing, finance, hospitality, e-business, the NHS and local government.

These case studies were selected to provide contrasting industries and labour markets. It was anticipated that this would highlight different issues and challenges for talent management.

Across the case-study organisations over 100 detailed face-to-face interviews were conducted with senior executives, HR directors, HR professionals, talent management specialists, line managers and individual employees. Employee focus groups added further information. Where appropriate, trade union representatives were also interviewed.

The aim was to obtain the views of a broad range of stakeholders on how talent is defined, identified and developed within their organisation, as well as their perceptions of the advantages and disadvantages of the approach taken. The stakeholders were at four levels:

❖ strategic level – led by the board and other senior executives as part of the strategic planning process

❖ policy level – the design and communication of talent management policies and processes

❖ practice level – the application and execution of talent management programmes

❖ experiencing talent management – the experience of being at the receiving end of talent management interventions.

The interviews conducted in the case-study organisations provided evidence from each of these levels. Thus, a combination of primary evidence from interviewees in a diverse set of organisations and other CIPD research led to a comprehensive portrayal of talent.

THE REPORT STRUCTURE

The resulting report presents the findings of the study and has been structured to provide information on the background to talent management in case-study organisations and others, to offer conclusions about strategy, stewardship and policy, and to highlight practices in the execution of talent management programmes. The structure of the report is as follows:

Chapter 2 – Understanding talent and talent management – explores what is meant by the term 'talent management' and how 'talent' is defined within different organisational contexts.

Chapter 3 – Talent strategy, policy and governance – places talent management within a strategic context, linking it to wider organisational strategy.

Chapter 4 – Talent management, succession planning and talent pools – examines the link between talent management and succession planning, and explores how individuals, and/or groups, are selected for talent management programmes.

Chapter 5 – Attracting talent – focuses on the recruitment of talent, and the importance of employer branding and strong organisational values in the process.

Chapter 6 – Developing talent – describes how various learning and development interventions, including coaching and mentoring, play their role in talent management.

Chapter 7 – Managing talent – highlights the importance of performance management processes and retention policies.

Chapter 8 – Who makes talent management happen? – examines the contribution of the key organisational stakeholders in talent management.

Chapter 9 – Tracking and evaluating talent management – explores the processes used in organisations for measuring the effectiveness of talent management .

Chapter 10 – Conclusions and practical implications.

It became clear that – at whatever level – a definition of what is meant by talent is critical to the success of any strategy that is put in place.

UNDERSTANDING TALENT AND TALENT MANAGEMENT

2

❖ **Successful talent strategy and practice depends on having a common organisational understanding of what is seen as talent, and a shared language for talent management.**

❖ **There are a wide range of approaches to talent management and no 'one right way'. But there are some common themes that stand out.**

❖ **Amongst these are a range of concepts which are particularly relevant. These include: the talent pool, talent pipeline, talent review panels, human capital and succession planning.**

WHAT IS TALENT?

The starting point for our research was to formulate a definition of what is meant by 'talent'. This was based on the premise that successful talent strategy and practice depends on having a common organisational understanding of what is seen as talent and a shared language for talent management. There is a wide range of views and opinions:

> *There are as many definitions of talent, it seems to me, as there are pebbles on Brighton beach! There's a lot of confusion around the place, and one of the things that we're trying to sort out here are the boundaries, such as 'Is there a definition that we can all be comfortable with?' and it's still not right. I define it as a positive psychology – it's a pattern of thought, feeling and behaviour that is associated with success on the job – and that's a bit esoteric for many people, but that's basically where we're moving towards. Then we worry about skills and knowledge and experience as a subset. So have people got a talent for the job, yes or no? If they have, then how can we develop and grow them in the context of that talent?*

> Director of People, Property and Assurance,
> Standard Chartered PLC

What emerged from the findings, in common with other studies, is that talent definitions were organisationally specific and influenced by the type of industry and the nature of its work dynamic. This need for common organisational understanding, and for a shared language that fits with organisational culture, means that not all organisations will wish to use the term 'talent management'. What is clear is that the objectives and the activities that take place are more important than the labels given.

> Organisations find greater value in formulating their own meaning of what talent is than accepting universal or prescribed definitions. There will be considerable differences, for example, in how talent is defined in a local authority and the hospitality industry.

Examples of the differences include:

❖ At Gordon Ramsay Holdings talent is essentially viewed as the creative flair of chefs.

❖ At Google, a person regarded as talented is referred to as a 'Googler', which is described as being confident, an 'ideas person' and a 'challenger who thinks outside the box'.

❖ At PricewaterhouseCoopers LLP talented individuals are those who possess 'drive, energy, an applied intelligence, a willingness to take on challenges and demonstrate the ability to make a distinctive difference to the business'.

Although the approaches may be different, two themes stood out.

The first is a medium- to long-term view in which talent is associated with those individuals who demonstrate the most potential to progress to more senior roles. These roles may be leadership- or management-based or in a different function or even discipline.

The second is more short-term, in which talent management is focused on attracting and retaining individuals to meet the immediate business needs at all levels.

The research also gave evidence of approaches taking place across a talent 'spectrum'. On the one hand there was an exclusive approach, in which talent is viewed on the basis of those destined for the top positions. On the other hand there was an inclusive approach, in which talent is defined as all the employees who work for the organisation. The reality is that most organisations had a hybrid approach to talent, in which both exclusivity and inclusivity are accommodated and indeed driven by the changing needs of the workforce. The implications of this are covered in more detail later in the report.

Three other features came out when looking at the question of the definition of talent.

The first is that talent potential tended to be based on personal performance and observed behaviours. As one talent manager put it:

> We see talent as a recurring pattern of behaviour which is associated with successful performance in a role.

Secondly, successful performance is a feature of those defined as having talent and is linked to four key characteristics. These were articulated as high levels of expertise, creativity, leadership behaviours, and initiative (see Table 3, below). These were those most frequently associated with talented individuals by interviewees.

Table 3 ❖ Characteristics associated with talented individuals	
High levels of expertise	Creativity
Leadership behaviours	Initiative

The importance attached to the different characteristics depends on the needs of the organisation and the nature of the work. The modernisation agenda of the public sector case studies, for example, required talented individuals who could demonstrate a combination of leadership behaviours and high levels of expertise. At Google and at Gordon Ramsay Holdings there was an emphasis on high levels of expertise, initiative and creativity. Talent in an individual is recognised to be a complex and dynamic mix of these key characteristics.

> We found a critical factor in defining talent is the presence of a shared understanding of what it means between the different parties in the employment relationship. Without this, the scope for misunderstandings due to different interpretations and a loss of employee engagement with organisational priorities is considerable.

The third feature from the research was that the mix of what is regarded as important varies according to, first, the sector in which the organisation operates; second, the type of work; thirdly, the customer orientation; and finally, the changing external and internal circumstances faced by the organisation.

In conclusion, the research has shown that a definition of talent in an organisation will take account of both long- and short-term needs, will depend on identified and demonstrated behaviours, and that successful performance of the individual will be key.

A working definition of talent that came from the findings may therefore be proposed as:

> Talent consists of those individuals who can make a difference to organisational performance, either through their immediate contribution or in the longer term by demonstrating the highest levels of potential.

Our research then turned to the definition of talent management and the execution of the talent management process.

> The extent to which the term 'talent' is used and communicated in policies and practice is a critical factor in developing shared organisational understandings of what is recognised as talent.

WHAT IS TALENT MANAGEMENT AND HOW IS IT IMPLEMENTED?

All of the organisations in our research had a common aim to ensure a supply of talented individuals, whether these were to meet short- or long-term corporate needs. The activities involved in developing this resource are the processes of talent management.

> We recruit bright people – people who have a natural 'giftedness' or talent that could be or should be useful to our business. Our business has the responsibility to try and help them realise that.
>
> Head of leadership, development and talent management, PricewaterhouseCoopers LLP

And common understanding in the case-study organisations allowed a further broad definition of talent management to be proposed as follows:

The systematic attraction, identification, development, engagement/retention and deployment of those individuals with high potential who are of particular value to an organisation.

Talent Management: Understanding the dimensions,
CIPD Change Agenda (2006)

This view is supportive of that by Baron and Armstrong (2007), who saw talent management as 'a comprehensive and integrated set of activities to ensure that the organisation attracts, retains, motivates and develops the talented people it needs now and in the future'.

However, our research has shown a further critical factor that should be explicit. 'Using talent' should also be a focus for talent management programmes.

> The effective deployment of 'talent' is a critical success factor to any talent management process.

Our research then turned to the implementation of talent management processes and showed that a fair number of approaches were identified across the spectrum. These ranged from management succession planning on the one hand to a comprehensive set of HR strategies and activities for attracting, identifying, developing, motivating, progressing and retaining high-potential individuals for immediate and future needs on the other; formal policies well integrated with one another on the one hand to a bundle of discrete practices on the other.

The findings of the CIPD's 2006 Learning and Development survey illustrated in Table 4, similarly supports the picture of 'a mixed bag' when it comes to talent management practice. It reveals that talent management is at a very early stage of development in many organisations if it is on the radar at all.

In spite of this there were some commonalities in those organisations where talent management was taking place. The case-study organisations use specific terms and refer to concepts associated with talent management. For clarity the most commonly used are summarised here.

❖ The *talent management pipeline* refers to the different elements that make up the talent management process which includes the acquiring, retaining, developing and managing of individuals identified as talented. The 'talent pipeline' can provide a framework to inform the design and application of systems for tracking talent and measuring talent management interventions.

❖ A *talent pool* describes a collective of talented employees who have been identified as talented. They can take different forms, have different memberships and be used for example as a means of resourcing project work, secondments and internal recruitment. In some organisations we encountered the practice of classifying different talent pools: one such example lists 'exceptional talent, rising stars, emerging leaders and local talent'.

❖ A *talent review panel* is a group of individuals drawn from across an organisation which includes representatives from senior management, line management and the HR function as well as individuals with particular expertise in the area. The responsibilities of the panel could involve reviewing the selection of individuals into the talent pool, tracking their progress, evaluating the success of talent management initiatives across the organisation and identifying areas for future action and adaptation.

❖ *Human capital management* is defined by Baron and Armstrong (2007) as the strategy used to analyse,

Table 4 ❖ Talent management adoption by sector and by size	
	% undertaking talent management activities
Sector	
Private sector	56
Public sector	46
Voluntary sector	30
Number of employees	
500 or more	61
250–499	54
100–249	35
Less than 100	35

Source: CIPD Learning and Development Survey (2006)

measure and evaluate how people policies create value for an organisation. This means it lies at the heart of talent management, which is about creating a flow of talent to ensure that it is available as a major corporate resource.

❖ *Succession planning* in the context of this report is used to refer to the planned replacement of key staff. Hirsh (2000) defines it as a management process by which one or more successors are identified for key posts (or groups of similar key posts) and career moves and/or development activities are planned for these successors.

❖ An *exclusive, inclusive* or *hybrid approach* to talent management is referred to in many of the case studies. This is one of the ways used to explain whether an organisation's approach to talent management provides an opportunity for all employees to be considered as a member of an identified talent pool or whether it is restricted to certain occupational groups or grades. This is also described as an 'egalitarian *v* elitist approach' or an 'open-access *v* restricted approach'.

The research into the definitions of talent and talent management has implications for practice.

IMPLICATIONS FOR PRACTICE

The study revealed that it was crucial to identify what the organisation means by talent and that this meaning fits its particular needs and circumstances. It is the starting point for developing a coherent talent management strategy. The following are some of the practice guidelines that might be used in this process.

❖ *Identifying potential* is the common denominator we found in most definitions of talent and has led to our suggested generic definition of talent as 'those individuals who can make the greatest difference to organisational performance, either through their immediate contribution or in the longer term by demonstrating the highest levels of potential'.

❖ *Identifying the characteristics of 'talent'* was a further critical step. The characteristics most frequently associated with talented individuals are identified as leadership behaviours, creativity, high levels of expertise and initiative. The nature of the industry and work roles are the major influences on these different characteristics, so it is important to understand how talent is defined within your own operational context.

❖ *Developing and communicating a common understanding of what is meant by talent* is the third implication for practice. The message from the study is that time invested in this will assist employee commitment to organisational approaches to talent management and reduce the potential for misunderstandings in the employment relationship.

❖ Finally, linked to the issue of a common understanding is *the importance of developing a shared organisational language* for talent management activities. Without this the scope for ambiguity is considerable, as we can see in the different terms used to describe the extent to which talent management initiatives are available to all employees.

These four factors were identified as critical to the early stages of any talent management approach that might be adopted.

This chapter has identified the importance of having an understanding of how the organisation defines talent, agreement on a common language and organisation-wide buy-in as the fundamentals for the platform of talent management.

Of course, the definitions are the first stage in the development of a successful talent strategy.

But what is a talent strategy, and how is this dealt with in the case studies?

TALENT STRATEGY, POLICY AND GOVERNANCE

3

✤ **Talent management is most effective when directly linked to corporate strategy and related objectives.**

✤ **Talent management also has to link directly to other HR processes.**

✤ **Preparation of individuals for senior management and associated leadership roles is the main focus of development activities in talent management.**

INTRODUCTION

In the previous chapter, definitions of both talent and talent management were described as the foundations on which the organisation would build its talent strategy. The key themes of talent management emerging from the research – such as the importance of defining talent in context, supply-and-demand features of the talent labour market, and different dimensions in the design of talent management policies – provide further groundwork in this process.

But a further area of critical importance was the need to put talent management in a strategic context, linking it to corporate and business unit strategy.

This was based on the view that an organisation's chosen strategy determines its approach to talent management. On the one hand the organisation will want to ensure a pipeline of top managers in its succession plan to lead its departments, business units and divisions during the period of implementation; on the other it will want to ensure that throughout the organisation there are sufficient talented employees to deliver against the key performance indicators (KPIs) identified for the success of the strategy. Whether the organisation has adopted an exclusive approach to the way it manages its talent (ie focusing on the top managers in the organisation, their immediate successors and a selective talent pool) or whether an inclusive approach is taken (ie where everyone in the organisation is assumed to be 'talent'), talent management and organisational strategy will be closely linked.

We regard talent management as a strategic activity... We're looking for talent now who can stay with us for the duration, to help us build the business and become more innovative in our product

development... This means linking our local and global HR and talent strategies with what's being planned by the board at corporate headquarters.

Human capital manager

Our research found talent management to be overwhelmingly seen as a future-focused activity in the case-study organisations. It was viewed as an investment in human capital aimed at meeting the strategic needs of the organisation in the longer term. As one Chief Executive observed:

We need to plan for the next generation of leaders and we need to give them real opportunities to develop their talents before the current senior management retires.

How talent management is approached at boardroom level sets the vision and the attention attached to it for the whole organisation. This is evident in the reported personal experiences of chief executives and directors in our case studies and in the CIPD 2006 Change Agenda *Talent Management: Understanding the dimensions*, which explores the links between corporate governance and managing talent. The Higgs Report (2003) identifies the importance of this link in its recommendation that building up talent among non-executive directors is vital for productivity.

Existing corporate and HR strategies shape the approach to talent management. Yet this creates a number of tensions highlighted by our interviewees. These are, though, by no means universal issues. In most, but not all, of our case-study organisations talent management is gaining in importance and attention. It seems that there is a long way to go, however, before it is widely recognised as a strategic imperative.

A particular concern for the public sector, for example, is how to accommodate the objectives of talent management within well established and communicated equal opportunities and diversity policies. Identifying and recruiting certain individuals into a talent pool for future leadership roles seems to be at odds with an open-access policy when it comes to opportunities for progression.

> We have a very long tradition here of going to the open market to ensure we offer job opportunities to the widest pool of candidates. This seems at odds with our growth of an internal pool of talent. We need to resolve which is our priority for developing managerial capability for the future.

In addition to the key drivers already highlighted, we found that interest in talent management was specific to the particular strategic challenges facing the case study organisations. For example:

✤ Cargill is investing in talent management to develop its future leaders and managers in the face of intensifying global competition for talented individuals.

✤ For the National Health Service Trust, obtaining and developing the skills and competences required to meet the demands of healthcare in the twenty-first century is paramount. But there is also a requirement for individuals capable of balancing the demand for services within the sector's resource constraints.

✤ In Derby City Council continuing changes in local government make leadership skills and managerial capability increasingly critical but difficult to find through external recruitment due to skills shortages and the sector's image.

✤ the rationale for talent interventions at PricewaterhouseCoopers LLP and Standard Chartered PLC are market factors – namely, client and customer demand. Both organisations report intense competition for talented individuals with the right skills and competences at all levels of the organisation.

✤ Creating a competitive edge, a strong reputation and rapid growth are the impetus for talent management at Gordon Ramsay Holdings. Achieving organisational success is dependent upon attracting and nurturing creativity and individuals with drive and initiative.

✤ At the Legal Services Commission there is an explicit strategy to develop leaders to support the organisation through a major change programme in the nature of its service delivery.

✤ At the London and Quadrant Group, the most important organisational objective lies in recruiting individuals who demonstrate the highest levels of organisational commitment and enthusiasm for delivering quality housing services.

✤ For Google the dynamic and unpredictable nature of the IT industry means that the overarching requirement is to attract and retain those individuals with the abilities to keep the business as a market leader.

Despite these variations, four main issues emerged across our case studies which require decisions about the strategic priorities of the organisation when considering approaches to talent management. These are:

✤ Budgetary constraints mean that difficult decisions have to be made about where the focus in talent management should be. A resource-based view of human resource management inevitably leads to a focus on the talents of a particular group or groups.

✤ How to combine the widest access to job opportunities and career progression in line with equality of opportunity policies and practices with the presence of an identified pool of talented individuals developed as a resource to fill key organisational roles.

✤ Initiatives to address identified under-representation of certain groups – for example, managers from different ethnic backgrounds or women in senior management positions.

✤ Planning for succession through talent management initiatives. A sufficient supply of talented individuals to fill key roles throughout the organisation is crucial. Such initiatives can be aimed at the future organisational leaders of departments, business units and divisions.

What the research showed was that the preparation of a talent strategy was not a neat sequential process but dynamic, changing and based on iteration, dialogue, challenge and response. So how does this show itself in practice, and what lessons can be learned about setting a talent strategy?

LINKING CORPORATE AND TALENT STRATEGY

In developing a talent strategy, both internal and external factors must be taken into account. Figure 2 on page 14 shows how these different factors and processes relevant to the strategic and operational dimensions of talent management are related.

Ensuring that talent strategy is closely aligned with corporate strategy has been identified in this model as a priority. In this approach, strategic analysis from the business perspective will inform the HR forecast and then the processes of talent management can be put in place based on both quantitative and qualitative conclusions from the forecast. It will be an iterative process with some key steps:

* *Strategic analysis*, which marries external and internal factors resulting in a corporate or business unit strategy. An outcome of this will be the people requirement informing the HR forecast:

  * identifying those corporate strategies that have implications on the demand for talent whether these are qualitative or quantitative
  * analysing external market supply potential
  * analysing internal supply potential.

* *Ensuring that the evolution of the corporate strategy has 'talent' inputs:*

  * HR to participate in corporate or business unit planning- input and output
  * Matching internal people capability with the external business opportunity.

* *Preparing an HR forecast based on this iteration:*

  * Translating the outputs from the corporate or business unit strategy with a demand forecast
  * Identifying potential sources of supply – internal and external.

* *Identifying where interventions for talent management will be needed and at what level:*

  * Quantitative requirements – *what numbers* are needed to satisfy the needs of the corporate or business unit plan?
  * Qualitative – does the organisation have the people with the *skills* to deliver to the corporate or business unit strategy?

* *Designing talent management programmes* to support the strategic analysis.

* *Building tools for the measurement* of the success of the programmes over time.

Evidence from the research has suggested that these links will be of increasing importance. Testing this hypothesis showed that in three of the case studies, talent management was part of a planned and systematic strategy. The experiences of these organisations are outlined later in the chapter. In others, a talent strategy was still in the process of development or discussion.

Given the iterative, evolutionary nature of talent strategy setting, the research highlighted some of the characteristics of both the formal, strategic approach and the less formal. There was no value judgement placed on whether one approach was better than the other, because it was evident that an organisation's strategic approach was evolutionary, stemming from where the organisation was in its own talent 'cycle'. What was clear, though, was that as talent management becomes an item on the CEO's agenda for board-level dialogue (Rubin, 2006), the demand for a strategy would increase. Most of the case-study organisations were aware how important it was that any talent management initiatives clearly flowed from corporate goals and the necessity for HR professionals to be involved in the corporate strategy-setting process from which the talent strategy would evolve.

One aspect that was evident about talent management was the heightened and sophisticated awareness and, at times passionate, involvement of the leaders of the case-study organisations. Mervyn Davies, Chairman of Standard Chartered PLC, highlights the many ways in which talent management can be considered an important strategic activity:

> Talent comes in many different forms – managing people, trading, good performance, creativity. I look for different skills and talents in my own corporate team and to see that they can develop their skills. You can nurture talent if there is a passion there.
>
> But there is a war for talent in international businesses so we have to be good at talent-spotting. You have to develop an intuition for spotting the right talent. This means taking risks – and the risks are high, as we operate in a lot of different markets, businesses and countries. You also have to learn from bad experiences.
>
> Here we have internal and external challenges. We are a high-growth company in a low-growth industry. How do we spot people around the world when I am based in London? As head, I am in control of the 'gene pool'. The external challenges are many. Internally the challenge is how to respond to identification of talent for growth, for cross-border work and operating in lots of different industries. In our talent management schemes we look to develop early network schemes for the young recruits coming from different parts of the world.
>
> I tell people that they will experience lots of highs and lows in their careers. They have to learn to survive the negative aspects, for the talented develop resilience. It's not so much about vision. It's more about delivering on everything. We've got a classification system here. We set clear objectives. Good people can do anything in different functions, different countries and different businesses.
>
> To align talent management processes you've got to have good processes. Talent management and human

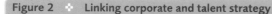

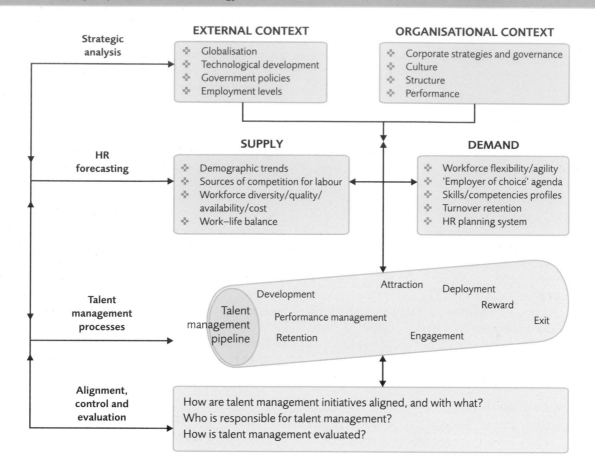

Figure 2 ❖ **Linking corporate and talent strategy**

capital management may be seen as boring processes but they are not just paperwork exercises. They are challenging, strategically important processes and you've got to have talented people in charge of these processes. Otherwise, it just won't work.

There is also a clear link between corporate social responsibility and talent management. If we are to attract the right sort or people from different cultures, we must be clear about how corporate governance links to corporate social responsibility and that our brand promises the sorts of values we stand for. One of the new phenomena of talent management is the importance of showing talent how we are linking profits to principles. We must also give people huge learning opportunities to grow, to have great experiences and to see the world.

We have more women in senior positions. The family structure is more important. We have more diverse secondments. These help our people become better at International project work and become more and more creative and less restricted in outlook.

The more you spend on talent the more you nurture

talent. If you don't have talent throughout the pipeline, you get short-term business performance – then you crash.

I don't count the time I spend on talent management. I see it as an essential part of my job. I meet our coaches and say to them 'Don't bring your own agenda. We don't want the latest fads. I want you to keep on message. Don't steer away from these.' Also, I have certain ways of getting to large numbers of our people. For example, I made a 'big call' to our top 100 managers this morning by video-link. Tomorrow I will talk to six managers in separate conversations.

Mervyn Davies, Chairman, Standard Chartered Bank PLC

The research has shown some characteristics of the process of developing a successful talent strategy. Links between talent management and corporate strategies were shown to be likely to occur in circumstances where:

❖ there are well-articulated corporate strategies which highlight the importance of talent to the organisation's mission

❖ organisation-wide commitment to shared values and corporate responsibilities is evident in all processes which have implications for talent management, such as recruitment and selection

❖ the head of an organisation publicly recognises the contribution that talented individuals make to the business

❖ there are processes for other members of the top team to gain a shared understanding with the head of the organisation on how talent shall be defined and resourced for the future

❖ the views of the senior HR director or specialist are listened to and acted upon

❖ appropriate resources are assigned to talent management processes.

It was felt that effort on the part of HR specialists with talent responsibility to ensure that these factors are in place in their own organisations would yield benefits when seeking buy-in, organisational commitment and, ultimately, resources.

Linking talent strategy to corporate or business unit strategy would inevitably lead to concerns about corporate governance. The research therefore tried to determine whether there were links and whether the corporate governance/talent dialogue takes place.

Given the recent emphasis on corporate governance, it is likely that people issues will assume a higher profile in many organisations and talent management will play a key part in this since the principles of good governance will impact on the approach to talent management. Corporate governance is concerned with the duties and responsibilities of an organisation's board of directors concerning shareholder accountability, directing managerial activity, and setting strategy. Having the appropriate supply of talent is important in each of these governance activities. Some conclusions are:

❖ Corporate governance will be a factor increasing in importance in the way in which 'top' talent is selected and developed – this might include those identified during the succession management process.

❖ Corporate governance will increasingly inform the way in which all employees of the organisation behave in their dealings with other stakeholders.

❖ In both, corporate governance should be explicit and measures put in place to track performance against them.

When questions about corporate governance were posed as part of the research, it was found that there was an acknowledgement of the relationship and a tacit understanding that the two were linked.

If we are to attract the right sort of people from different cultures, we must be clear about how corporate governance links to corporate social responsibility and that our brand promises the sorts of values we stand for. One of the new phenomena of talent management is the importance of showing talent how we are linking profits to principles.

Chief Executive Officer

However, for many, forging the links between talent management and corporate governance was an evolutionary process.

The CIPD research has shown evidence of talent management being dealt with as a strategic issue, including references to corporate governance, but the approaches are not consistent. Factors that determine the approach taken by a specific organisation include the status of the organisation in terms of its own growth cycle; the type of market in which the organisation operates; and the nature of the labour market in the organisation's business sector.

So what happens in organisations that have a well articulated talent strategy – and those that do not?

FORMAL TALENT STRATEGY OR INFORMAL, EMERGENT STRATEGY

The previous section looked at the approaches to setting a talent strategy in the context of the overall corporate strategy. The outcome will either be a set of formalised talent strategies or a less formalised, more emergent view. How does this hypothesis translate when looking at the case studies, and can they provide insights into the different choices to be made in selecting an approach to talent management that is appropriate to the needs of the organisation? The research showed that there was once again a spectrum when it came to determining talent strategy. At opposite extremes of this were 'no strategy' and 'well-articulated strategy'.

The identified key dimensions that emerged are illustrated in Figure 3 on page 16.

The first key point relates to the presence of a talent management strategy. The evidence suggested there was a link between the status of the talent strategy and the sophistication of the talent. The extent of a coherent and articulated strategy is heavily influenced by the stage of development of talent management practices. The evidence from the case studies in fact showed four levels of development:

Level 1: Talent is managed in an ad hoc way with no formal practices or strategy

Level 2: Some formal practices, but still no overall strategy

Figure 3 ✧ **Stages of development of talent strategy**

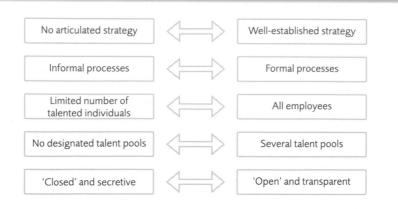

Level 3: Formal practices and limited strategy applicable to one segment of the organisation

Level 4: Joined-up formal practices linked to an articulated strategy linked to a wider corporate strategy.

There was evidence of good practice at all levels, so once again there is no 'one best way' of undertaking talent management, but there were several case-study organisations aiming to move through the stages – in other words, making the transition to a more formal, strategically-integrated approach.

Three of the case-study organisations have:

✧ clear talent management strategies and policies

✧ an identified goal of including all groups of employees in their talent management activities

✧ a systematic identification of specific talents necessary for the future success of the organisation

✧ policies to enable the development of employee potential

✧ formal processes which are made known and linked to other HR processes

✧ continual reviews of their talent management interventions.

Other organisations were found to operate in a less structured way. This does not mean that they are unaware of the need to respond strategically to their changing organisational context. For example, North West Wales NHS Trust is one organisation which is becoming increasingly strategic in its approach to talent management and reflects an organisation moving through the stages as outlined above.

Case study 1:

FORMALISING TALENT MANAGEMENT IN THE NORTH WEST WALES NHS TRUST

The Trust covers the North Wales counties of Gwynedd and Ynys Mon as well as parts of Conwy, serving a population of around 240,000 and transient/seasonal workers and holidaymakers in the summer months. Direct provision of health services is undertaken in two acute hospitals, nine community hospitals and two sites for mental health and learning disability services.

Key drivers for talent management within the Trust

The Trust is affected like other public sector organisations by national government policies. In its case, this directly includes the Welsh Assembly Government as well as indirectly the UK Department of Health. These policies directly and indirectly influence both the internal need for and the external availability of talent. The 'business' of the Trust also means that there is great variety in the nature and type of talent demanded by its services. These include leadership, managerial, clinical, technical and administrative talent as well as that associated with the extensive and specialised facilities found in hospitals.

The complex mix of skills and competences required to meet the demands of health care in the twenty-first century is one key driver for talent management. Another is the requirement to achieve service provision and meet demand in the context of tight resources. The essential resource in health care is, of course, human and so talent management is critical. It requires the most efficient and effective contribution possible from employees.

How the Trust is approaching talent management

The Trust currently adopts an informal approach to talent management. The term itself is not widely used and does not appear in formal and official policy statements and documents. There is, though, a clear and well developed HR strategy which gives effect to talent management in practice. There is also a deliberate attempt to create conditions that foster talent management practices and to develop a culture which reflects the aspiration to be a learning organisation. In that sense, the main focus of talent management can be said to be learning and development rather than recruitment and resourcing.

Although there are central initiatives managed by the HR function, the main thrust of talent management seems to be decentralised with directorates and departments within the Trust taking responsibility for managing talent. Considerable use is made of secondments to assess and develop talent, and other semi-informal methods such as mentoring and coaching are also utilised. Corporate policies and central HR initiatives seem to be intended to support and supplement activities at directorate and local levels. A current example is application of the NHS-wide Knowledge and Skills Framework (KSF) which is being implemented alongside a new performance management system. The latter emphasises personal development planning and is fully integrated into the appraisal process and provides the main focus and outcome of policy and practice. The process is known as Personal Development Review (PDR) to signal and reinforce the development orientation and purpose of the policy. The process is directly linked to the KSF, and the link to 'gateways' which facilitate progression in pay grades provides a connection with promotion and reward management.

The latter link also enables a focus on career development, both laterally as well as vertically, through development and application of transferable skills and skills of relevance and value in alternative roles. The Trust reinforces this message with an explicit statement in the PDR policy document:

KSF should be used to inform career development planning as well as development within a post. Career progression and development might take place by moving up levels in the same dimension or by adding

on different dimensions as individuals move into new areas of work. Directorates are requested to consider the effectiveness of facilitating/funding relevant training to enable internal staff to develop their NHS careers as an alternative to the recruitment of external staff.

The PDR process follows the well established framework of preparation (which includes evidence collection and gathering to demonstrate application of KSF dimensions), annual review meeting, formulation and agreement of a PDP and then implementation of the PDP. A six-month progress review meeting forms part of the process and such meetings can be more regular if appropriate. It is not a requirement that reviews are conducted by an individual's line manager and the policy documents refer to 'reviewer' rather than 'manager'. Both policy and guidance documents emphasise the various forms and methods of development and so reinforce the message that development does not necessarily mean 'courses'. The range of additional and alternative methods advocated includes:

✢ involvement in projects

✢ one-to-one coaching/supervision/mentoring

✢ use of local learning resources/programmes

✢ use of learning zones/Internet/technology

✢ taking on a new area of responsibility/ secondment/shadowing

✢ visits to external sites

✢ networking and professional contacts

✢ shadowing a colleague in another discipline, specialty, directorate, etc

✢ external personal development which adds to individuals' skill-set

✢ e-learning, reading periodicals/journals, etc.

This is not to say, though, that courses – including those that lead to qualifications – are not encouraged. A related and supporting policy governs decisions about support for such courses and, as the statement above indicates, qualification-based development is encouraged and supported within the Trust. The alternative methods do however reflect the ambition to become a learning organisation and the related ambition of seeking continuous improvement through continuous learning.

The aim in the Trust is that each and every employee from the Chief Executive to a hospital cleaner holds and owns a PDP. If realised, such an aim will certainly help in relation to most aspects of talent management, including identifying and tracking talent. The latter will be achieved by the Trust's decision to utilise the national 'e-ksf' electronic tool as part of its PDR process.

The issues and challenges of talent management in the Trust

A major issue is the complexity created by the variety and diversity of talent needed to deliver high-quality healthcare services. Such delivery depends on cooperation and collaboration between employees drawn from a wide range of professional and technical backgrounds, and on being able to plan and allocate resources to achieve the required balance and blend of talent. Another issue is the geographical location of the Trust. This can be a benefit in recruiting from the local population where there is little competition. It can equally be a disadvantage in recruiting more widely from national and international populations. This mostly applies to scarce and specialised clinical skills. However, even here the Trust does have advantages which include the very attractive physical surroundings and the close links with the University of Wales, Bangor, which facilitate both teaching and research opportunities.

Another major challenge is that of resources. Although financially stable, the Trust is not cash-rich and so has to manage expenditure on talent management carefully. This is perhaps reflected in the value attached to the efficiency as well as the effectiveness of less formal approaches to and methods of talent management more widely as well as those of learning and development. The mix of and relative autonomy of functions and related directorates is another challenge. This relates in part to identifying, monitoring and tracking talent across the Trust. As indicated above, this will be facilitated in future by the NHS KSF initiative. An additional challenge is that of developing leadership. The Trust participates in external initiatives and programmes such as one aimed at nurses, and is currently developing its own internal management/leadership development programme. An interesting aspect of this issue is the notion of 'service leadership' being worked on in the Trust. This is to supplement the established association of leadership with managerial and clinical roles.

What the benefits have been so far

One major benefit so far of the informal approach adopted has been the development and internal promotion of a number of employees. An interesting example is that the Trust currently has three senior executives, including the Chief Executive, who have progressed through the organisation and have personally benefited from being 'talent managed'. Some of these, including the Chief Executive, have held posts elsewhere as well as with the Trust, but all started their careers there. There are, however, many other examples at lower levels, and so identifying, developing and nurturing talent clearly works in the Trust. A feature of this is both vertical progression in a profession or function and horizontal moves into new and different departments and functions.

An additional benefit is a high level of commitment to continuous personal and professional development among managers and employees. It would be wrong to say that this is universal, but it certainly seems to be more widespread than is often the case in large organisations. It is notoriously difficult to specify and so assess progress towards becoming a learning organisation. Widespread commitment to learning and development is, though, generally acknowledged to be a feature of learning organisations, and so the Trust can claim some foundation for its declared aspiration.

The dynamics for linking talent strategy to both corporate strategy and corporate governance are growing stronger. It is proposed that a talent strategy that is aligned with its corporate strategy will have a greater chance of being communicated and understood throughout the organisation, making the process of buy-in easier. Evidence from the case studies suggests that in some organisations at least there is a move from informal to an emerging strategy and a well-articulated strategic approach linked to the overall corporate strategy.

The evidence for aligning talent strategy with corporate strategy and the reasons for so doing are compelling. Where organisations do this and receive sign-off for the development of a talent management programme, however defined, the work of ensuring that this is joined up with other HR processes will begin and the move from strategy to execution can take place.

Cannon and McGee (2007) in the CIPD's *Talent Management and Succession Planning* Toolkit suggest that the beginning of the process is to establish a business case for devoting resources to the talent management activity. Using tools such as human capital management to demonstrate a clear link between organisational goals and the talent required to deliver them will help to make that case. At this point in the design of the talent management programme it will be important to ensure that links are in place with other aspects of management development that the organisation has established.

There was evidence that in case-study organisations attempts were being made to identify the key processes of talent management so that a more structured approach could be introduced, and indeed so that the processes were supportive of each other. This might be summarised as a talent management 'loop' as outlined in Figure 4.

| Figure 4 ❖ The talent management loop |

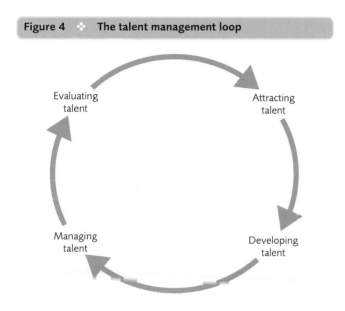

This is the beginning of the transition from strategy to implementation and each of the activities identified above is dealt with in subsequent chapters. Before doing this, however, we must deal with a fundamental point of who should be included in talent management programmes.

IMPLICATIONS FOR PRACTICE

❖ *Aligning talent strategy with the corporate or business unit strategy* is an important critical success factor. This involves identifying those corporate strategies that have implications on the demand for talent; analysing external market supply potential, and analysing internal supply potential.

❖ Similarly, *ensuring that the evolution of the corporate strategy has 'talent' inputs* by HR's participation in corporate or business unit planning.

❖ *Ascertaining where interventions for talent management will be needed*, and at what level, will inform the talent management process.

❖ *The drivers for talent management depend on the sector and the nature of work*, but these change over time so an organisation's talent management activities should be kept under regular review to ensure that they are still meeting corporate needs.

❖ *HR and talent management specialists must keep abreast of changes* in the external labour supply and use this intelligence to support the development of approaches to talent management.

❖ *Building tools for measurement* of the success of the programmes over time is something that is increasingly required in organisations.

TALENT MANAGEMENT, SUCCESSION PLANNING AND TALENT POOLS 4

+ **Defining talent in the organisation will inform the decision about which people should be included in talent management processes.**

+ **There are advantages and disadvantages in choosing an inclusive or exclusive approach to talent management.**

+ **Talent management and succession planning are linked processes, and a joining up of both will yield benefits.**

+ **Talent pools are often a characteristic of talent management.**

INTRODUCTION

In the evolution of the approaches to talent management we have identified key stages and activities:

+ a definition of talent that has organisation-wide buy-in

+ a definition of talent management and how it will be approached in the organisation

+ strategic analysis matching the talent strategy to corporate or business unit strategy and taking into account corporate governance

+ a review of approaches to talent management to ensure that they are consistent with the broader approach to development and joined up with other HR initiatives.

But the question to be answered now is who should be included in talent programmes at any given time. The research looked at how this is dealt with in case-study organisations and what conclusions could be drawn.

The strategic analysis of current and future talent needs will have produced both quantitative and qualitative information to inform decisions about talent types and numbers. The research suggested that most organisations had a hybrid view of talent that combined both exclusive and inclusive approaches and this would inform the choice of participant in any talent initiatives. However, it is worth considering the advantages and disadvantages of choosing a particular definition at the extremes of the talent spectrum.

There are implications for talent strategy where talent management is seen to be focused on individuals whose

Table 5 ❖ The pros and cons of an exclusive approach to talent management	
Pros	Cons
+ provides an identifiable, strategic resource for succession planning if aimed at the future leaders of the organisation	+ high potential for reduced engagement and increased turnover among staff not included in a designated talent pool.
+ targets finite resources – financial and non-financial	+ less scope to increase diversity
+ more opportunity to offer individualised development programmes to the talent pool	+ reduced development opportunities and resources for employees not on a talent programme
+ easier to track and evaluate the benefits	+ if focused upon one occupational group or grade, other types of talent may be overlooked

Table 6 ❖ The pros and cons of an inclusive approach to talent management

Pros	Cons
❖ wider employee engagement if the entire organisation has access to a talent pool	❖ learning and development and other resources are spread too thinly
❖ supports succession planning place for all key roles, not just senior management	❖ increased competition for progression which requires managing
❖ encourages the development of a more diverse workforce	❖ individuals with skills core to the business may receive less investment, to the detriment of the organisation's strategic goals
❖ more opportunity to benefit from all the talents of the workforce	

performance indicates high leadership potential and who are placed in an elite sub-group of future leaders for the organisation. Concentrating exclusively on a targeted few rather than taking a more inclusive 'whole workforce' approach has both advantages and disadvantages, as shown in Table 5 on page 21.

At the other extreme, talent management programmes that adopt a more inclusive approach reflect a view that a broader spectrum of employees has talent to offer the organisation. The case for a more inclusive approach that is not just based on one of increasing diversity is made by Bones (cited in Warren, 2006, p.25), whose argument is that greater competitive advantage is achieved when all the available talent in a workforce is fully utilised. But there are again reported advantages and disadvantages to this approach as shown in Table 6, above.

The case-study organisations felt, in principle, that talent management programmes should be made available to all employees. In reality, resource constraints and business priorities meant that such programmes were often limited in their application. A hybrid approach was both a compromise and a practical alternative. Adopting an inclusive approach was identified as a particular interest in the public or not-for-profit sector. The Legal Services Commission is an example of an organisation that has moved quickly to the decision to extend its scheme – with all grades of staff able to apply – as a result of reviewing its current approach.

Case study 2:

TALENT MANAGEMENT IN THE LEGAL SERVICES COMMISSION

The Legal Services Commission (LSC), established under the Access to Justice Act 1999, is the executive non-departmental public body which replaced the Legal Aid Board in 2000. It reports to the Department for Constitutional Affairs with a remit to maintain and develop the Community Legal Service and Criminal Defence Service through which legal and advice services are funded in England and Wales. The core purpose of the LSC is to help people in genuine need to gain access to justice, and it works in partnership with solicitors and not-for-profit organisations to provide legal advice, assistance and representations. A further responsibility of the Commission is to identify unmet need for publicly-funded civil legal and advice services and develop suppliers and innovative services to meet identified priorities.

At the time of the study the LCS employed 1,700 staff working in 12 offices in regions across England, one in Wales, and a London Head Office. It also operates eight Public Defender Service (PDS) offices where staff are directly employed to deliver criminal legal aid. In 2005–6 the LCS delivered over 708,510 acts of assistance through the Community Legal Service and 1.6 million acts of assistance within the Criminal Defence Service.

The key driver for talent management at the LSC

The rationale for growing talent internally at the LSC is the need to retain individuals with high potential to support the future development of the organisation at a time when changes in how legal aid are provided are impacting on the Commission's services and its staffing structure. It is increasingly important for the Commission that its managers possess broad transferable skills and are effective at working in third-party relationships. A combination of difficulties in recruiting to certain senior posts and a lack of internal applicants led to a decision at the LSC that there had been too high a reliance on buying in external talent and more ought to be done to 'grow their own'.

The approach to talent management

The Commission is in the early stages of its talent management programme, which was developed and designed by a group of stakeholders drawn from around the organisation including members of the executive team. The programme is supported by a talent panel which consists of two executive board members and three other directors, including the HR director, and an independent member who was the development consultant at Roffey Park and had contributed to the design and development of the programme.

The Commission's internal publicity about the talent management programme describes it as

a flexible and transparent framework that identifies people for future key roles, and provides opportunities for them to deliver the LSC of the future and to enable them to fulfil their potential and take responsibility for their careers. Our immediate focus is on using talent management as a succession planning tool. The Executive Team has said our first priority is to identify those who can replace them and future members of the Senior Leadership Group, and to provide these people with the career development tools they need to get there.

The Legal Services Commission's approach is one of inclusivity but in the first cohort of their programme operated an exclusive approach in that only 11 individuals had been selected from applicants from three of its four salary bands. It was intended to make it totally inclusive by being available to all salary bands by including Band A for the second cohort.

The selection criteria for the programme focused on two key elements: first, to find individuals who were high-performers in their current roles; and second, to identify those with the potential to go further within the organisation and who had a desire to do so. An individual had to display both of these elements in order to be considered eligible for the programme. Each business unit had been asked to complete a Talent Audit assessing the performance and potential of everyone within the unit at Band B and above. Candidates in this band were encouraged to apply if they felt the programme was right for them, that it fitted in with their career plans, and that they were able to give it the commitment it would require.

This approach highlighted an issue common to other case studies about the challenges of what form of talent management programme should be developed – an exclusive or an inclusive mode? Several

envisaged a shift over time from an exclusive focus on the leadership team, then other key positions, then, over time, perhaps to the rest of the population in the organisation.

The benefits so far

There was a shared view among the different interviewees that the talent management scheme had revealed new talent within the organisation through its very open process. This was regarded as an improvement on the previous system, described as a 'tap on the back' approach, in which opportunities had tended to be limited to well-known familiar faces.

Participants on the programme were highly positive about their experiences and felt that although it was a high-risk strategy in terms of investing in just a small group of individuals who were being made more employable, the demonstrable commitment the organisation had shown to them had increased their organisational commitment.

While recognising that there was still work to be done in measuring the value of the talent management programme, the members of the talent panel who monitored and evaluated the programme reported that the process had allowed 11 of the most able people employed by the Commission to come forward and be developed for future succession. This was not to say that there were not other equally talented people in the organisation with the potential to develop, but the process was at an early stage. The programme had demonstrated that there were very capable people internally who had the potential to grow, and one director saw a demonstrable success in the number of them that were

beginning to run quite quickly and are beginning to understand what makes the difference between a relatively low-grade manager in organisations like this and a senior manager taking control of their own development... Some of these people are now beginning to make a difference in the organisation...

Issues and challenges

As the first programme was implemented, some interesting debates emerged in relation to the influence of talent management design on the inclusion and exclusion of talent. As individuals chose whether or not to apply, a number self-selected themselves out – for example, following recent promotion or because of existing work commitments

– and there was a concern that defining any group as the talent pool might be seen as suggesting those not included were less talented. Some managers were concerned that vital but limited resources for development were now focused on a privileged few whereas a wide coverage might have a greater organisational impact. The talent panel acknowledged that the engagement of line managers in the talent management initiative was an area where more work must be done.

The LSC had initially identified the programme as being for individuals who were 'capable of progression by two salary bands within two to three years', which had led to an expectation that some managers felt would be difficult to deliver. Related to this was how opportunities for promotion would be handled as they occurred. Having singled individuals out as capable of rapid progression, not to deliver on this when opportunities arose was seen as unfair, yet there was the issue of access to promotion opportunities for other internal applicants.

Another challenge was that the programme was essentially self-led, based on individual personal development needs and not formally structured. This approach was intended in the design of the scheme and was supported by a heavy investment in developing a coaching culture across the organisation which was an important source of support for the talent management programme. Notwithstanding this highly individually tailored current approach, it was recognised that extending the programme to include Band A applicants was likely to mean that elements of the programme would have to become more formalised.

The Legal Services Commission case study reveals how a carefully staged talent management process can bring benefits, where lessons can be learned at each stage and a robust strategy begins to emerge. This case also shows the type of questions that can usefully be asked when making decisions about how people gain entry to a programme. They include:

❖ How is the talent management programme communicated to employees?

❖ Do individuals self-select or are they nominated?

❖ Who nominates individuals for programmes?

❖ What selection methods should be used, and who should be involved?

❖ To what extent should the focus be on developing internal talent?

PERFORMANCE, POTENTIAL AND INDIVIDUAL MOTIVATION

The Legal Services Commission selection criteria for its programme (identifying both current high-performers and those with the potential to go further) highlights an important area in regard to the criteria organisations choose for entry onto specific programmes.

Some use regular performance reviews (or development centres) to plot where they believe the employee sits on performance/potential matrix (Figure 5).

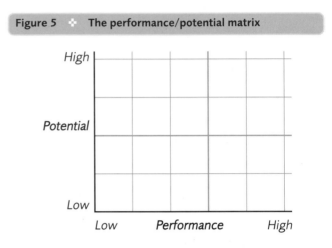

Figure 5 ❖ The performance/potential matrix

Some organisations go further and plot tranches of employees on this matrix to help with their resource planning.

It is important to remember that it may not just be those employees in the top right-hand quadrant who are of interest in terms of talent management. For example, if you have taken a risk with a 'talented' individual and given him or her an early promotion – he or she may not yet be performing highly but still have high potential.

Equally, if you are looking at talent management to ensure that key roles (for example, of an operational or technical nature) in your organisation are filled, it could be that it is 'solid performers' you need in these roles.

The Legal Services Commission case study also demonstrates the need to identify those who have aspirations to progress in the organisation (bearing in mind, for example, their own motivations, preferences and other commitments outside of work). This requires good-quality conversations between individuals and managers – an area this report considers in greater detail in Chapter 7.

Table 7 ❖ The pros and cons of a focus on internal talent	

Pros	Cons
❖ growing internal talent can help address skills shortages in the external labour market	❖ selecting talent internally can reinforce an organisational lack of diversity
❖ recruiting internally during major organisational change demonstrates that talented individuals must be retained during a difficult time	❖ internal recruits may just be 'more of the same' when there is a need for new thinking and innovation
❖ there can be less risk in internal recruitment to a talent pool because more evidence is available about individuals	❖ consideration must be given to accessing 'entry-level talent'
❖ identifying talent internally recognises the aspirations of employees	❖ it may be difficult to provide sufficient opportunities for progression to meet expectations
❖ recruiting internally sends out positive messages to individuals that their skills are valued	
❖ costs are lower than external recruitment	

DEPLOYING INTERNAL TALENT EFFECTIVELY

The drivers discussed earlier led the majority of case-study organisations to place a greater emphasis on the development of talent within their current workforce through internal recruitment. A number of advantages and disadvantages to recruiting talent internally are apparent from our research. These are described in Table 7, above.

There seem to be rather more arguments for an internally-focused approach to growing talent, but it is important to acknowledge that the available level of skills and specialist expertise is the major consideration. The value of internal recruitment is, however, evident in this director's comment:

The introduction of talent management may initially have been related to some recruitment difficulty, but really it seems such a shame that if you have got people in-house that are capable of progression – if we don't give them the help – then we need to take the risk with external people... When I have recruited externally, I have always struggled. All my successful recruitment has been internal.

The director of human resources in the same public sector organisation raised a similar issue:

About two years ago we advertised a quite senior management position and we got no responses at all from within the organisation, so we ended up making an external appointment. This ends up with a situation where you are worrying about sending a very negative message internally when you are

always going to the external market when senior appointments come up.

The identification of talented people, by whatever definition, raises another dimension, and that is the way in which talent is structured. We found that talented individuals are usually organised into groups that are called 'talent pools'.

THE TALENT POOL DIMENSION

'Talent pool' is the term used to describe a collective resource of talented employees. Talent pools can take different forms and have different memberships. Employees are placed in a talent pool through a variety of methods including the normal performance review process, 360-degree appraisal, development centres and line manager nomination. It is important that there is transparency in the selection process for talent pools – a point made in several of our case-study organisations. Of equal importance is the fact that talent pools are dynamic entities. They flex and change depending on business requirements. The case-study organisations ranged in having:

❖ several designated talent pools with different memberships

❖ just one designated talent pool

❖ no formally designated talent pool but nonetheless a pool of talent built up as a result of talent management activities.

Google has a 'universal talent pool' with different 'streams', reflecting its inclusive, 'open to all' approach to talent management. For example, one stream consists of the customer services staff who make up the majority of employees. Another stream is IT specialists who develop new products. Google relies heavily on this creative talent to keep the business innovative and competitive.

A number of the case studies targeting the development of future leaders had a categorised hierarchy in their talent pools – as the organisational example from the banking industry that is Figure 6 illustrates.

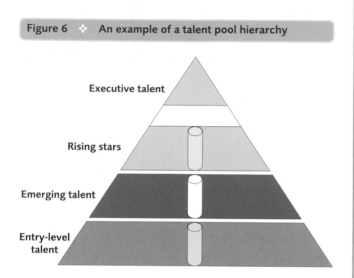

Figure 6 ❖ An example of a talent pool hierarchy

Another trans-national organisation has specific talent pools aimed at different levels of staff which are reviewed regularly. These are currently:

❖ business leaders who are seen as future Chief Executives

❖ a pool of about 30 mid-career hires to provide a source of new talent thinking and perspectives

❖ a pool of 40 MBA recruits from key business schools globally, which will increase to around 80

❖ an international graduate pool of 262 graduates recruited for an international assignment as a precursor to a fast-track career under a very rigorous selection route

❖ a talent pool made up of high-potential women to help address issues of diversity within the organisation.

The Cargill case study below illustrates a similar approach.

Case study 3:
TALENT POOLS IN CARGILL

Founded in 1865 as a single grain elevator in the United States, Cargill now serves five key international customer segments – crops and livestock, food, health and pharmaceuticals, financial and risk management, and industrial – and has annual sales and other revenues of approximately US$75.2 billion. Cargill employs more than 149,000 employees in 63 countries and is continually growing, particularly in eastern Europe, China and Asia. Its employees work across a wide range of areas including fields, laboratories, offices, production facilities and trading floors.

Key drivers for talent management within Cargill

Because Cargill's businesses grow in countries with different challenges, its need for talented leaders and managers will rise and change over the next five years. Like so many other international organisations it is already facing stiff competition for key staff in different economies across the world, and this will only intensify in the future. Internally, Cargill's corporate talent management team is driving talent management through rigorous design and implementation strategies, with an increasingly integrated approach. Whereas talent management used to relate either to recruitment, performance management or development, it is now about using all three to achieve the best results. The growth of talent management from all of these initiatives is also driven through solid executive board support and an awareness of how closely talent management initiatives must be linked to the goals of the organisation.

How Cargill is approaching talent management

The company offers a variety of opportunities for entry-level recruits, senior-level professionals and enthusiastic individuals in all roles. Cargill's talent analysis is organised into different 'pools'.

Gerardo Soula, human resources director in South America, explained how Cargill's talent pools are structured:

We have 'leadership' and 'talent' definitions for the corporation that are applicable on a global level, no matter what geography or Cargill business you are in. Cargill has a Leadership Model that is used by all

businesses and functions to assess their talent. There is a group of selected employees – those we name NGLs (Next Generation Leaders) and Corporate NGLs (Corporate Next Generation Leaders) – that are included in what the company defines as 'the corporate pool'. This group is made up of approximately 300 leaders, and our top leaders in the organisation are responsible for the development and careers of this group.

Identification and development of emerging leaders within our business units and functions is key. We define Emerging Leaders as high-potential employees that have the skills and behaviours required to be the future leaders of the organisation, but they still need to be stretched in order to obtain experience and exposure to challenging assignments.

Another category in our talent definitions is High-Impact Performers (HIPs). HIPs consist of those employees who are consistently high-performing 'thought leaders' whose departure would slow business unit/function strategy growth. My responsibility is to ensure that there is a process in place to identify and develop the talent in the region, and to ensure that we fill any gaps in the talent pipeline, either by developing our existing employees or by recruiting the talent from the external market.

There has been a global talent management initiative in Cargill for several years which is reviewed frequently. Cargill has devised a corporate Talent Statement around what it means to be a part of the senior-level talent pool. Representatives from the different parts of the world where the company has businesses meet twice a year to consider how talent might be managed and succession planned in those businesses as they inevitably change over time.

The issues and challenges of talent management in Cargill

In a global organisation with several different types of businesses, a Cargill HR director may have responsibility for between 1,000 and 4,500 employees. For example, HR director Martin Earnshaw manages human resources for some 3,200 employees in Europe in Cargill's businesses producing industrial starches and high-intensity sweeteners, from the refining of corn or wheat into starch and sweeteners products. He describes talent management in Cargill as the identification of people with both the ability and potential to rise in the organisation. Once these have been identified, attention must be given to their development and

how they are moved around the businesses to fully utilise their talents. He says,

We operate at a local level, a European level and a global level. In driving the business forward, most of our senior people in the business have European or global responsibilities, and our development policy reflects this. Employees with leadership potential are gaining cross-cultural awareness through working in different parts of the world, as well as intensive career and self-development. The great challenge for us going forward is that we are increasingly becoming a much wider-spread business operating on a European or global base, so we need to ensure we have the right talent with not just business but also cultural awareness.

Another Cargill HR director, Jos Zwienenberg, is responsible for human resources in Cargill's cocoa and chocolate business, which has around 1,250 employees in several countries around the world. As for Earnshaw, one of Zwienenberg's major challenges is managing staff mobility across the globe to run plants in geographies that are often outside an employee's experience in terms of skills, knowledge of the culture and area and language capability. This also means that tracking changes of employees' job details, training, career aspirations and movements is a vital strategic consideration for the organisation.

What the benefits have been so far

The development programmes for Cargill's different talent pools – such as the Next Generation Leaders and Emerging Leaders – involving both formal and informal development, are reaping rewards in terms of encouraging the leaders of today and tomorrow to think and act globally as well as locally for the good of the business as well as developing their own careers.

In Cargill's Leadership Academy, entrants learn about the fundamentals of leadership and management in the company and work through a number of accelerated leadership modules gaining the global knowledge to enable them to lead Cargill businesses in different countries. All of these courses are interspersed with more challenging projects and work assignments where participants work with supervisors and managers in different Cargill businesses and countries. Cargill corporate leaders also take part in a Leadership Academy, where they learn transformational leadership skills and the essentials of coaching and mentoring in formal programmes and informal learning activities, all of which form an important part of their leadership

> development. Coaching and mentoring processes are considered a key aspect to strengthen talent management programmes for the future.

The research shows a number of learning points for those organising and managing talent pools. These are summarised in the Learning Points box below.

THE RELATIONSHIP BETWEEN TALENT MANAGEMENT AND SUCCESSION PLANNING

The CIPD's factsheet on succession planning cites Hirsh's definition of succession planning as 'a process by which one or more successors are identified for key posts (or groups of similar key posts), and career moves and/or development activities are planned for these successors'.

Succession planning was frequently mentioned by senior managers as the purpose of their talent management

initiatives, and we found that specific differences between talent management and succession planning are not always clear in practice.

A complication is that the terms could be used interchangeably in those case studies where the prime objective was to develop future leaders for the organisation – for example, where the age profile of senior executives has led to planning for their succession becoming the focus of talent management. At times it seems that 'talent management' is regarded as a more fashionable term for what was previously known as succession planning. It is an important learning point to be clear about what the objectives of both talent management and succession planning are, and what the reasons are for investing in them.

One view, however, is that talent management is a more dynamic process than succession planning, which makes it better suited to the uncertain environment facing today's organisations. Developing a talent pool is a broader activity than succession planning. Put another way, talent management interventions can provide a wider organisational resource to support succession planning, which is specific in its focus.

LEARNING POINTS FOR TALENT POOL MANAGEMENT

There should be clear criteria when selecting a highly aspirational group with expectations of progression. In one case study, entry to the talent pool has initially been presented as individuals 'capable of progression by two salary bands within two to three years'. Certain line managers feel this is overly ambitious.

Some talent pools are more strategically important than others. In Gordon Ramsay Holdings senior chefs constitute a particular talent pool which is distinctive from the general restaurant staff. When discussing 'talent', chefs are mentioned most often, which suggests a 'hierarchy of talent' based on scarcity of skills. Although restaurant staff are vital in terms of customer service, they are more easily replaceable in the labour market.

It is important to have progression opportunities for those in the talent pool. Several organisations face the issue that once individuals have been developed as talent, not to deliver on progression will fail to meet individuals' expectations. For example, Derby City Council recognises the need for a planned next stage for a talent pool of 70 individuals who have completed a Leading Manager programme.

There must be consideration of equality of opportunity and diversity in career opportunities. Public sector organisations have a commitment to open access to all jobs, so giving special opportunities to a talent pool may challenge long-established principles of equality and diversity. Talent management initiatives also have to take account of identified areas for action such as a lack of women in the senior management team and the under-representation of ethnic minorities in managerial roles.

Designated talent pools must be carefully managed. In the NHS Trust they found that the idea of a designated talent pool is problematic because of its commitment to equal opportunity, diversity and an inclusive approach to talent management. A different view is expressed by a manager in Gordon Ramsay Holdings who points out that 'You can't have an organisation full of talented people.'

Talent pools need regular reviews to ensure their continued relevance to the business. Several of the case studies regularly review the structure and membership of their talent pools to ensure that organisational needs are continuing to be met.

As a process succession planning has a number of distinctive features.

❖ Succession planning is a complex process with many levels and layers (Giambatista *et al*, 2005). The focus of succession planning tends to be on the *most senior* of staff, such as the CEO, members of the board or other key senior organisational positions, but is not exclusively so. It depends on the nature of the work.

❖ Because they are concerned with the long-term health of the organisation, the CEO and the executive board must lead the way in ensuring that succession planning is undertaken appropriately. This means that it is a process that must be aligned with talent management initiatives.

❖ Traditionally, succession planning is associated with career moves for identified individuals in a highly structured way. As Hirsh (2000) points out, this is a model that is more appropriate to a stable environment and career structures.

❖ Succession planning may have constraints such as a lack of transparency.

❖ It can present particular issues for the public sector who have long-established open-access approaches to job opportunities.

Notwithstanding succession planning frequently being associated with senior roles, a number of interviewees suggest that it should be used for key roles at all levels of the organisation, and that it is not just about vertical progression. As one HR manager observed:

We have always thought about succession planning in terms of the top of the organisation, but on-going difficulties in recruiting to some key posts lower down the organisation suggest that we need to have a radical rethink.

Talent management can be seen as a 'feeder' process to succession planning. But a lack of thinking through the relationship between succession planning and talent management can clearly cause problems. Once again, the need to join up talent management processes with others within the HR sphere is emphasised.

Each case study reveals a variation in its approach to the relationship between talent management and succession planning. This depends on the organisational drivers for talent management. In our local government case study, talent management is considered in terms of succession planning.

Case study 4:

SUCCESSION PLANNING AND TALENT MANAGEMENT AT DERBY CITY COUNCIL

Derby City Council (DCC) is rated by the independent Audit Commission among the best local authorities in England and Wales and has been awarded a four-star status. It works closely in partnership with other agencies that provide services for the 237,000 people who live in Derby city, which is home to international companies such as Rolls-Royce, Toyota and Royal Crown Derby. The Council has been a unitary authority since 1997 and employs some 12,000 people.

A new organisational structure of five directorates of Children and Young People, Environmental Services, Regeneration and Community, Resources, and Corporate and Adult Social Services was introduced in 2006 under the leadership of the Chief Executive. Developing leadership skills has been picked out as a key issue for the organisation, resulting in a new Leadership Charter and a 'Leading Manager' programme which is designed and delivered jointly with the local university. The Council is beginning a senior manager coaching programme to address leadership needs at first- and second-tier levels of management.

Key drivers for talent management within DCC

The main rationale for growing talent at DCC is succession planning and stems from an identified need to develop managerial skills and experience within the organisation. This is largely due to the age profile of senior staff and the demographics of the wider labour market which is perceived as likely to reduce the numbers of talented individuals attracted to local government in the longer term. Due to a long-established principle of recruiting through external as well as internal advertising to promote equal access to Council job opportunities, there has not been a tradition of internal succession planning.

In terms of growing talent, the Chief Executive has determined that the Council requires

more managers with generic management skills as opposed to more technically competent people. It has been the problem of local government that people tend to get promoted through their professional and technical competence, and that is not always what we are looking for.

The approach to talent management

A talent pool of over 70 employees has been created through the successful completion of a well-established Leading Manager programme run by Derby University in conjunction with the Council. Achieving a place on the programme is a combination of self-selection and local management support, and is not the result of an organisationally-led planned selection process.

What the benefits have been so far

The Leading Manager programme has resulted in a pool of aspirational individuals who are keen to take on new challenges and play a part in moving the organisation forward. For most of them the reality has been a continuation in their current job role, but it is recognised that the potential that has been developed should be better utilised. One of the benefits of the initiative has been the growth in awareness of the senior management team that these employees must be better deployed for the benefit of the organisation and the individuals themselves.

The importance of the Council's 'Achievement and Development' process as the central hub of its approach to planning individual development and the value of coaching as a core managerial skill to support talent management are increasingly being recognised and have formed part of the new HR strategy for the authority. This is reflected in a planned shift in approach, away from simply attending courses to a greater emphasis on self-development, coaching and mentoring, using secondments, project-working and shadowing as the means of developing the potential of its workforce.

Issues and challenges

A major issue for DCC is that, in common with much public sector employment, it has had a commitment to open access to all jobs through external advertising. On the one hand, giving special opportunities to the managerial talent pool that has been developed challenges long-established principles and practice on equal opportunities and diversity. On the other, it is recognised that the talent pool has to be utilised – otherwise, it will be detrimental to employee retention and motivation. It is also acknowledged that there must be a proactive approach to developing existing internal capability to address the current lack of women on the senior management team and the under-representation of ethnic minorities in managerial roles.

Budgetary constraints are a key concern, and there is a view from some respondents that spending on the Leading Manager programme uses up very limited central resources when general supervisory capability is the vital concern for organisational performance. It has also been noted that the role of the immediate line manager is pivotal in spotting and nurturing talent.

In summary, this chapter demonstrates that there are a number of internal and external factors driving interest in talent management and that many of these factors are influenced by the organisational context. These steps provide a framework for talent management, and the challenge of acquiring the right levels and quality of talent will follow.

IMPLICATIONS FOR PRACTICE

❖ *Talent management strategies must take proper account of both external and internal factors* affecting the availability of talented individuals to meet corporate needs in the short and longer term. This requires a proper audit of the organisation's environment as the first stage in the process.

❖ *The decision to have an exclusive or inclusive approach to talent management* has implications for both the level of resourcing and the nature of talent managment programmes.

❖ *The relationship between succession planning and talent management activities has to be properly thought through* and communicated across the organisation.

❖ *Areas where there are potential conflicts in talent management and other HR policies and practices must be identified* and addressed as part of determining strategic priorities.

ATTRACTING TALENT 5

- ❖ **The ability to attract external talent depends upon how potential applicants view the organisation, the industry or sector it operates in, and whether they share the values of that organisation.**

- ❖ **The creation of an attractive 'employer brand' is a factor in attracting external talent.**

INTRODUCTION

The previous chapters were concerned with strategic approaches to talent, linkages with other development initiatives and the whole question of who should be included in the talent pool of the organisation. We now turn to the question of how strategy can be turned into practice.

A first arc on the talent management loop illustrated in Figure 4 (see page 19) is the attraction of talent. In this chapter we examine some of the potential challenges employers may face when trying to attract talented individuals to their organisation, particularly those individuals who have key skills or professional, technical and/or leadership potential. In many cases the problems seem to be the same as reported in recruitment more generally, as highlighted in the CIPD's 2006 Recruitment, Retention and Turnover survey.

A lack of specialist skills is identified as the major recruitment issue for employers by the CIPD's 2006 Recruitment, Retention and Turnover survey, with the situation in the public sector reported to be getting worse. In common with other studies, our research reveals that the biggest variation exists between public and private organisations in respect of attracting and recruiting talent. Local government appears to face particularly acute problems in terms of attracting talent (SOCPO, 2005).

> *We had to start growing managerial capability. It is going to become increasingly difficult to find what we need to take us forward by external recruitment. Everyone is looking for talented managers – and they are in short supply.*
>
> Head of HR, local government

With regard to managerial talent, the local authority case study attributed recruitment difficulties partly to image but also to a traditional emphasis on service expertise, rather than on leadership and management capability.

The research reveals that the ability to recruit external talent is influenced by:

- ❖ the image of the industry or sector as a place to work

- ❖ the image of the organisation as a place to work

- ❖ the extent to which potential employees identify with the organisation's values.

The first of these areas is the importance of the image of the industry or sector in which the organisation is active. How did this affect the acquisition of talent?

INDUSTRY OR SECTOR IMAGE

The research showed that the image of the industry or sector as a place to work can have a positive or negative impact on an organisation's ability to attract talented individuals.

Operating in a high-profile private industry tends to enhance an organisation's ability to attract talent, particularly if the industry is associated with 'specialist talent' such as Google, Gordon Ramsay Holdings and PricewaterhouseCoopers LLP. In contrast, those organisations operating in the public sector – such as the Legal Services Commission and Derby City Council – report difficulties in attracting individuals with professionally recognised roles or 'specialist expertise', such as accountants, lawyers and surveyors. This is attributed to the private sector being able to offer a more attractive financial package. As an

HR manager at the London and Quadrant Group explains:

It's been particularly hard to recruit surveyors because we're in competition with the private sector in that area. They are able to pay the going rate. We're trying to do everything within our constraints, but that doesn't match what you can get within the private sector – especially if you're good.

The pay and benefits offered by public sector organisations are often perceived to be inferior compared to the private sector. In the NHS, for example, we found that they had difficulties attracting talent because of an inability to increase the salary being offered due to national agreements.

To offset this, the North West Wales Trust has as two strategic aims: 'to be the local employer of choice' and 'to be a learning organisation'. Staff development in the Trust is therefore treated as a priority and the Trust experienced very few problems trying to attract talent.

One of the key factors in attracting talent is the importance of the employer brand.

THE EMPLOYER BRAND

The image of an organisation as a place to work – more commonly known as 'employer branding' – is generating increasing interest from HR specialists and has a clear relevance to talent management. Creating an organisational identity that is regarded positively by current and potential employees can be an effective way to 'win the war for talent' (Edwards, 2005; Ulrich, 1997). The case-study organisations had an awareness of employer branding and its role in attracting talented people:

We all agree it's vital that we have an international corporate identity and brand values that have meaning internationally. That's what most clients expect as a minimum. We get that through great marketing and through our strategic deployment of people.

Our future business, market penetration, influence in the forums that count and profitable growth depend entirely on individual territories leveraging the brand in their local markets – we do that already. We make best profits and secure future business from maintaining our quality brand, and that depends on fielding quality people in the place they can make the most impact .

The ability to attract talent is influenced by how the employer is perceived by prospective employees. We found that those case organisations that have a prominent and high-profile position in their industry can attract talent relatively easy.

In corporate branding terms, Google is perceived as a 'celebrity firm' that takes a bold step in creating a distinctive identity and who is well regarded and widely known in the industry (see Martin and Hetrick, 2006, pp22–3). This has meant that it is able to overcome skills shortages in its local labour market in Dublin by attracting talent from 42 different countries. Having an internationally recognised employer brand is therefore advantageous in attracting external talent.

The results of a recent survey of those responsible for recruitment summarised in Figure 7 indicate that employer branding is important for organisations.

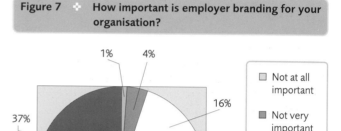

Figure 7 ❖ How important is employer branding for your organisation?

- Not at all important
- Not very important
- Fairly important
- Very important
- Extremely important

1% 4% 16% 37% 42%

Source: Willock (2005)

A strong employer brand combined with a dominant presence in the market can help to create a strong, attractive image for potential candidates.

To be seen as an employer of choice and to win the war for talent we undertake branding and recruitment activities where we try and clearly present an image of the organisation that communicates to potential employees, current staff and our customers our organisational values.

HR manager

Possessing a strong employer brand can counteract the negative image potential applicants might have of an industry. This is the case at Gordon Ramsay Holdings who, despite operating in the demanding hospitality environment, are well positioned as a key player in the sector. As their HR director explained:

We get a lot of speculative CVs just because of who we are.

Recruiting talent is also made easier when the organisation's image is enhanced as a result of public recognition of its work. For Gordon Ramsay Holdings, having restaurants with Michelin star status plays an important role in attracting talent. One senior restaurant employee's comment illustrates this:

I wanted to work for a Michelin star restaurant and get that experience under my belt, so I sent my CV here.

We found that other case organisations were less fortunate. Being poorly placed in a sector because of a weak employer brand means that it is difficult for these businesses to attract talent, particularly if it is not clear what is good about working for the organisation.

Clarity around the organisation's core activities is also important to attract talent. In other words, people seem to be reluctant to apply for a job in an organisation where it is unclear what it does. A lack of familiarity with an organisation can therefore deter people from applying. As one graduate remarked:

The main problem we have is that our profile affects recruitment and retention. When I was asked to work here, I hadn't even heard of [this organisation].

Cargill, in particular, experiences such problems despite being a multi-million-dollar international operation. Until appearing in the *Sunday Times* Best 100 Companies To Work For and the *Sunday Times* 100 Best SMEs To Work For lists, the London and Quadrant Group and Tower Homes (part of the Group) also experienced similar problems. The housing sector struggles to attract talent because the general public has limited knowledge of the nature of its work. Furthermore, potential applicants view it as dull and lacking in excitement, which means that working for a housing company is not a career choice for many people. As one manager stated:

Ultimately, I think that people don't really know what a housing association is. Is it public? Is it private?... They have to entice people and even sell what they are doing – which is not what companies often have to do.

The appearance of London and Quadrant in the *Sunday Times* lists has created considerable employer brand exposure and increased the number of applicants for key roles in the Group.

So having a strong employer brand can create a number of advantages for talent management:

✢ It can help to 'win the war' for talent by attracting the best candidates from the labour market.

✢ Individuals who share the values of the organisation will want to work for the organisation.

✢ It can help counteract a negative image of the industry as a place to work.

✢ Potential applicants will understand what the organisation stands for, making them the employer of choice.

✢ It can help support retention and high performance.

But a strong employer brand does have to be constantly reviewed and refreshed, and in addition the resources kept up to date, to ensure that the brand values continue to be delivered.

Industry or sector image and employer branding are important features of the ability to attract talent. A third related factor is the ability to identify with the organisation's values.

IDENTIFYING WITH THE ORGANISATION'S VALUES

The extent to which potential employees identify with the values, goals and mission adopted by the organisation is a feature of talent acquisition. Edwards (2005), for example, has commented on how graduates are increasingly taking into account the degree to which organisations are socially responsible.

> If the organisation is able to communicate its values clearly to the labour market, it is in a better position to attract talented individuals who share similar principles to those of the organisation.

The research showed that this is particularly true for the case organisations that have altruistic tendencies, such as the Legal Services Commission and the London and Quadrant Group. Working for what is seen as a 'just cause' helps to build a positive perception of these organisations amongst prospective employees. Due to the nature of their contribution to society, such organisations are able to attract talent away from large, profit-driven corporations.

For Google, attracting talent that shares the organisation's cultural values is also vital. Google has less typical organisational objectives which reinforce its corporate personality. These include:

✢ You can be serious without a suit.

✢ You can make money without doing evil.

✢ Great just isn't good enough.

Although an applicant's qualifications and experience are important when recruiting talent, the degree to which a person can be identified as a 'Googler' is crucial.

An HR specialist at Google explains the types of qualities their applicants should have:

> What we're looking for is a different person, not a traditional person... It's a 'Googler'. A 'Googler' is a person who is different, who doesn't think traditionally and doesn't take everything for granted. They want to challenge things, have done interesting things or worked really hard at something – and they've achieved it.

Recruiting appropriate talent that shares the organisation's vision means that all applicants to Google typically have to go through between six to eight selection stages. To root out prospective 'Googlers', unconventional questions are asked of those applying for technical positions. These include (Vise, 2005):

❖ In your opinion, what is the most beautiful maths equation ever derived?

and

❖ This space is left intentionally blank. Please fill it with something that improves upon emptiness.

Other organisations, such as the London and Quadrant Group, have different challenges. Yet because of the organisation's societal focus they are able to attract employees with similar values within their tight local labour market.

Case study 5:

EMPLOYER BRANDING AT THE LONDON AND QUADRANT GROUP

Established in 1963 to tackle homelessness in London, the London and Quadrant Group's main objective is to offer high-quality affordable housing to people in Greater London and the south-east of England. This includes providing accommodation for key workers, offering sheltered and supported housing and building and refurbishing properties. Its mission is to 'Create places where people want to live'. Like other housing associations, it is a not-for-profit organisation that is run by paid staff but supervised by a voluntary management committee.

London and Quadrant manages over 43,000 homes and has over 800 staff across 30 locations in the region, including its London head office. In 2006 the

Group's turnover was £183 million. This makes it one of the largest housing associations in the UK. In 2005 the Group was ranked twelfth in the *Sunday Times* 100 Best Companies To Work For list.

Approaching talent management

At the London and Quadrant Group, 'talent' has an inclusive definition – that is, talent management initiatives are open to all, and little distinction is made between different types of talent, such as specialist, creative or managerial talent. The term 'talent' or 'talent management' is rarely used in the organisation, and they do not have a formal talent management programme or strategy. Instead, talented individuals are regarded as having an enthusiastic and efficient approach to their work. This idea is also closely related to the organisation's values and mission. This is the belief that if employees are well trained and content at work, they are more likely to provide a better service for their clients.

Much of the emphasis in the L&Q Group is on developing talent internally rather than recruiting exceptionally talented individuals, partly because of the negative perceptions potential job applicants have of the industry as a place to work.

Employees are regularly appraised by their line managers, and this provides a suitable forum to manage the individual's talent. As one employee commented:

> The one-to-ones are excellent because on a monthly basis you're taking stock of where you are, what you can improve, how you can progress – so there's a real focus on evaluating what you're doing at the moment.

As part of the appraisal, shadowing and mentoring opportunities are organised across the Group in order to develop an employee's skill base. Line managers therefore play a crucial role in identifying and developing talent in the organisation.

The employer brand

In previous years the Group has experienced problems when trying to attract talent. Convincing prospective employees, especially graduates, that working in the public sector is an appealing proposition has been challenging. Competing for specialist talent with large privately-funded organisations, including those in the City, is difficult for the London and Quadrant Group because the corporate world is perceived to offer more exciting, better-paid jobs even though the organisation offers an array of benefits. In particular, the organisation has had difficulties in trying to attract surveyors away from private industry.

To make matters worse, outside the industry few people understand what a housing association actually does. Despite this, the philanthropic activities of the organisation – such as offering sheltered accommodation, providing accommodation for key workers and running community projects – means that it has had some success in trying to attract people away from the private sector.

The real turning point in its ability to attract talent, however, was when the London and Quadrant Group was publicly recognised as a good place to work. For three consecutive years the organisation has appeared in the *Sunday Times* 100 Best Companies To Work For list. In 2005 they were ranked twelfth. Furthermore, in 2006 Tower Homes – a subsidiary of the Group set up to help people buy a property – was placed first in the *Sunday Times* Best Small Companies to Work For.

These awards instantly boosted their employer brand by signalling to prospective employees that it is an employer of choice. It also helped the Group to 'win the war' for talent in the tight labour market. According to its HR director, appearing in the *Sunday Times* list has meant that

we get many more applicants now because people want to work for a top employer.

Similarly, a line manager commented that being in the list has made the Group more competitive in terms of acquiring talent. She said that appearing in the list

makes a difference to recruitment, because you're being identified alongside the private sector and not just within the public sector.

L&Q's current approach to managing talent internally has also created some interesting dilemmas. Many respondents view their line manager's involvement in managing their development positively, but some noted that if a manager decides to block their progress it is difficult to go elsewhere for support. Training line managers in managing talent and implementing transparent talent management processes is therefore vital.

Benefits

Developing talent internally means that the Group has been able to overcome recruitment problems in areas where professional, specialised skills are required. By offering surveyor training to female administrators it has not only addressed the skills shortages within the organisation but has also developed staff who were in non-professional positions. Furthermore, employing women in roles traditionally occupied by men has led to a positive impact on the diversity profile of the workforce. An emphasis on employee development has also led to a decrease in labour turnover, which has been extremely beneficial to the organisation given that frequent job changes are typical of those working in London and those employed in the housing industry.

Research has shown that there are several important characteristics for success in the first part of the talent loop – acquiring talent. Industry or sector image, the employer brand and the perceived values of the organisation are critical.

IMPLICATIONS FOR PRACTICE

There are a number of implications from the various approaches to the acquisition of talent as outlined above:

❖ The research showed that *the image of the industry or sector as a place to work* can have a positive or negative impact on an organisation's ability to attract talented individuals.

❖ *Having a strong employer brand* can create a number of advantages for talent management.

❖ *Understanding the organisation's position in the sector* is important and assessing the impact of industry sector 'brand' on the external labour market will be necessary.

❖ A further action will be to *assess the current employer brand* and determine the changes necessary to attract external talent.

❖ Which will lead to *building an employer brand to maximise positive and minimise negative effects* of the industry image. Use opportunities for high-profile and impact events such as industry awards and HR-related prizes.

❖ Where needed, *counter low financial rewards with alternative benefits and employer values* such as social responsibility.

❖ *Project clear messages about the nature of the business and operations as well as core values and beliefs.*

DEVELOPING TALENT

6

✤ **Linking talent development to other learning and development initiatives is desirable.**

✤ **Formal and informal approaches are used in talent development.**

✤ **Coaching of talent is increasingly used.**

✤ **Mobility and assignment to projects are innovative talent development opportunities.**

HOW LEARNING AND DEVELOPMENT IS USED IN TALENT MANAGEMENT

The second arc on the talent loop illustrated in Figure 4 (see page 19) is talent development.

Having acquired talented individuals, by whatever definition, it will be necessary to put in place effective talent development processes. Our research found a wide range of options were being implemented as part of talent development.

For example, the CIPD 2006 Learning and Development survey notes that:

✤ In-house development programmes, coaching and succession planning are the most common activities for developing talent.

✤ The most effective practices are in-house development programmes, internal secondments and coaching.

✤ External secondments and action learning are considered the least effective.

The survey also reported that 94% of respondents agreed that well-designed talent development activities can have a positive impact on an organisation's bottom line, and that developing high-potential individuals (67%) and growing future senior managers (62%) are the two main objectives for talent management activities. However, research suggests that a workplace culture in which people can maximise their potential is still not the norm, and this can affect their efforts in their job or cause them to look for opportunities elsewhere. Each can have a serious impact on organisational performance.

When you talk about talent development programmes, you are talking about helping people achieve even more than they are doing now. Sometimes it will be supplementary training around basic softer skills, but a lot of it is around 'stretch'.

One challenge for all organisations is to create the sort of environment where:

✤ the development of talent is supported

✤ talent management has clear links to the organisation's business strategy

✤ employees have opportunities to expand their learning experiences

✤ there is 'joined-up' thinking in combining the different elements of the human resourcing process.

Traditional ideas about career progression continue to be challenged as talented individuals are taking greater account of the ways in which their employer supports the development of their skills and capabilities. This is seen by Verhaar and Smulders (1999) as part of the 'employability' component in the new psychological contract between employers and their employees. The implicit deal is that those selected for talent development programmes maximise their learning opportunities for the benefit of the organisation as well as themselves.

PricewaterhouseCoopers LLP is an example of an organisation that has worked hard at achieving the balance for the organisation and the individual in the learning and development provision for talented individuals.

Case study 6:

TALENT DEVELOPMENT AT PRICEWATERHOUSECOOPERS LLP

PricewaterhouseCoopers LLP (PWC) employs more than 140,000 people in 149 countries on industry-focused services in the fields of assurance, tax, human resources, transactions, performance improvement and crisis management. It provides solutions to the problems facing businesses and the capital markets today through its lines of service and 22 industry-specialised practices for a variety of clients. Its aim is to continue to be the UK's leading professional services firm by investing in its people, supporting local communities and helping to shape its industry and rebuild public trust in corporate reporting. With 14,000 partners and staff in offices around the UK it draws on the knowledge and skills of its people in the UK and other countries in the global network of firms. Its strategy includes being the leading professional firm in the markets it decides to serve and being a great place to work for all its people.

Key drivers for talent management within PricewaterhouseCoopers LLP

Key drivers are both the need to address development requirements of all staff and the demand from clients for consultants with the right skills. Because the organisation is divided into different businesses, the possibility of having human resources in 'silos' of different disciplines is recognised. Efforts are therefore made to have an enterprise-wide view of the business and encourage the mobility of staff which is so important for both individual experiential learning and organisational development. Taking this approach matches what its clients want, which is having people at a senior level in client accounts who have experience in a number of sectors. This is so much more meaningful and useful to a client than having someone who has been in one sector all his or her life.

How PWC is approaching talent management

PWC has around 1,000 graduates, 650 of them in its assurance business. As a leading employer in the UK professional services sector, PricewaterhouseCoopers recruits highly educated junior professionals in the creation of its Level 1 talent pool. Its carefully targeted selection systems place new entrants on a structured orientation, training and education programme, undertaken over a period of four years. In subsequent stages, projects, secondments and work assignments aid experiential learning, develop required skills and enable the participants to gauge which areas of work they would like to settle in.

PWC presently has a global framework of seven core competencies which are the benchmark against which employees are measured for a variety of roles as they go forward. It is using those partly as definitions of talent and future leadership potential and partly as a statement of what might be called 'price of entry'. In the early stages its talented people have to have a relatively good level of expertise against these competencies, but when seeking leadership later on, PWC is looking for something that is not particularly embodied in the generic competencies used across the business.

The issues and challenges of talent management in PWC

Because of legislative requirements built into PWC's recruitment policies and graduates' subsequent educational development, technical competency is taken as a given. Other attributes are then majored upon, such as adaptability – but finding evidence of such qualities is one of the talent management challenges.

Its traditional way of training graduates has been by time-fixed movements through career stages, but it is beginning to develop more radical approaches within the constraints of legislative requirements and the required pace of movement through the pipeline. This involves the creation of work placement opportunities to build individual development through movement around the organisation. In this it is attempting to be responsive both to the individual and his or her personal desire for experiential learning and satisfactory pace of career development, while at the same time addressing organisational needs in terms of meeting job requirements and encouraging mobility to develop breadth of skills.

At the more senior level, mentors and coaches are perceived as important elements of executive development. As James Chalmers, assurance partner recounts:

The mentor role varies across our business. Some people will have structured mentor schemes, which can be less effective. Everyone should have the opportunity to have a mentor: they should explore who the right mentor is and they should be self-

starting. It is not necessarily one mentor. I have four or five mentors, depending on the circumstances or the situations I am in. They are a disparate group. I could list the people I talk to today but they might not be the same people I would talk to later on this year or next year.

Finally, PWC is aware of the necessity of gathering the right sort of talent management data and making it more readily available to those involved in the talent management process at all levels – not only to business leaders but also to its 'stewards of talent', who are senior partners from various parts of the business whose responsibility it is as part of a talent review group to look at the talent pipeline and report to the business leaders.

What the benefits have been so far

The essential element which helps PWC align organisational and individual needs is a structured performance management process which allows regular feedback and enables, when appropriate, speedy mobility between businesses, roles or tasks. The importance of including training in the development of emotional intelligence is also highlighted, and here different kinds of qualities are sought, such as listening empathetically, understanding one's own feelings, being emotionally stretched, and relating effectively.

Openness and transparency about people's potential to progress in the organisation is appreciated by PWC employees.

FORMAL APPROACHES TO TALENT DEVELOPMENT

In the talent management process many larger organisations make extensive attempts to clearly link career progression with appropriate learning and development interventions. This relationship can be see in Figure 8 below.

Figure 8 shows how different development processes are being used at different talent pool career stages. Several of the case-study organisations had similar hierarchical career structures for their talent pools, with similar interventions at each level. For example, Standard Chartered PLC had four types of investment:

❖ formal educational programmes for new entrants to the organisation which provide essential qualifications and 'core skills' for a role, such as an accountant

❖ formal educational programmes which reflect the needs of 'emerging managers', for example MBAs

❖ individual work projects, group task force assignments, sabbaticals, etc, to stretch individuals and help them develop key skills

❖ support from coaches, mentors and sponsors at various critical points in an individual's career.

In some of the case-study organisations formal educational provision was in collaboration with external educational institutions.

❖ PricewaterhouseCoopers LLP had a close relationship with a leading business school and also with other leadership academies

Figure 8 ❖ **Learning and development interventions in talent career stages**

Table 8 ❖ The pros and cons of a formalised, structured approach to talent development	
Pros	**Cons**
❖ a more formalised approach can enhance the organisation's ability to attract new recruits	❖ a more formalised approach can be inflexible
❖ it shows those in talent pools and their managers a clear, staged learning strategy linked to appropriate development processes	❖ the more diverse the talent pool, the greater the need for different development paths
❖ an interlinked set of processes supports the tracking of individual development and progression	❖ there may not be the scope to address a talent shortfall if individuals leave a programme at a particular stage

❖ Derby City Council's Leading Manager programme was delivered by a local university

❖ the NHS Trust also worked closely with its local university on nurse education.

Other cases, such as Cargill, had their own leadership academies which provided management and leadership development, and Google's aim was to construct 'a creative campus of talent'. In yet other organisations, the onus was upon individuals to demonstrate that they were interested in career progression and to undertake their own further education or training to develop key skills and competencies.

As would be expected, highly formalised and structured forms of developing talent have advantages and disadvantages. These are summarised in Table 8 above.

So having structured learning and development interventions linked to talent management appears to offer much in the way of clear strategies, policies and practices, but there are limitations for developing talent. We can see this in the following observations:

> *We lose bright graduate recruits that come in because we are a hierarchical organisation – we do tend to plot out very careful career paths from Band A1, 2, 3 to Band B1,2, 3, etc. We need to find good people for the A and B grades and be able to accelerate them, and I think we should concentrate the programme on that level.*

> Executive director

> *If you look at the new hires further up the career ladder, people will say that those who have come in from outside have been effective with their diversity of experience. But I also suspect it is harder for external people to progress at the same pace as those joining at the beginning of their career. I know there are people who have joined later on who have been*

> *successful, but it is harder for them to excel because they are coming in to the business with a skill where we are probably market leaders and already have trained people...*

> Talent development manager

In addition to the more traditional approaches involving courses and formal education, there were a range of exciting examples of how to get the most benefit from talent development. One of these was the increasing use of coaching.

TALENT COACHING

It is clear from these findings that less formal processes, such as coaching and secondments, have a particular value in talent development. The survey showed that 79% of respondents reported using coaching processes. This extensive use for talent development purposes was matched by our case studies. Coaching was used widely in Cargill, PWC, the NHS Trust and Standard Chartered PLC. As Jos Zweinenberg, HR director of Cargill states,

> *When you become a senior manager, you get a coach as part of the Cargill leadership development programme.*

The research highlighted some key learning points when it came to the subject of talent coaching:

❖ High-potential individuals must have their potential unlocked and be fast-tracked to retain their engagement. They can be coached through this process in a number of areas – for example, emotional intelligence, technical expertise and the ability to perform beyond their cultural comfort zones.

❖ Appropriate organisational coaches should be identified and trained with support systems set up for their management. As the CIPD Coaching Supervision event

Report (2006) suggests: 'Even the most experienced coaches need help to constantly re-examine their practice, to continue to develop their skills and self-awareness, and to avoid being drawn into their clients' systems.'

❖ The purpose of coaching should be clearly communicated so that all stakeholders are made aware of its purpose and what is involved.

❖ Talent coaching should be linked to development and performance management processes.

❖ There should be different coaching considerations for individuals in different talent pools – for example, for future leadership roles, coaching by senior executives is particularly relevant.

❖ Coaching should be an embedded part of the organisational and talent management culture.

In short, coaching in talent management has to be viewed as a strategic tool, and coaches should be well briefed by their employing organisations on its role in talent management interventions. As this company chairman points out:

I meet all our coaches together once a year and say to them, 'Don't bring your own agenda. We don't want the latest fads. I want you to keep on message. Don't steer away from these.'

Chairman

Formal and informal mentoring is another popular means of development in talent management. In some organisations individuals have additional support from 'sponsors'. In others, line managers operate as a mentor and, in some cases, a sponsor. Mentoring is often combined with internal secondment where a previous line manager continues as a mentor and/or sponsor and the new line manager as coach.

The NHS Trust HR practice is a good example of an approach which is less formalised yet combines a range of development methods such secondment, mentoring and coaching for the benefit of both employees and employers. It also illustrates that development activities do not have to be labelled or defined as talent management for that to be the effect.

That said, some organisations value clearly defined roles – as the quotation below shows.

A textbook would say that a mentor is somebody who is not necessarily in the line of reporting, but is somebody with the experience to be a good sounding-board or adviser and is really somebody, if someone's got a problem or wants an independent or neutral person, they can bounce things around on and talk to them and get advice. A sponsor is

someone who has a vested interest in making sure that an individual succeeds and can help them think about their future and make the future happen for them. A mentor cannot necessarily do that. We try to assign a sponsor to different categories of staff. Our international graduates have a sponsor; our emerging leaders have a sponsor. If you are in one of these well-defined talent pools you are likely to have a sponsor ...a manager who will take an interest in your individual learning plan and your career development.

Group Head of Talent Management and Leadership Development, Standard Chartered Bank PLC

Coaching is therefore a valuable tool in talent development. In addition, other innovative approaches were identified as part of the research.

MOBILITY AS A LEARNING AND DEVELOPMENT PROCESS

Employee mobility can affect the success of both formal and informal approaches to learning and development. The ability and willingness of individuals to move to different physical locations is often a factor in applying work shadowing and secondments, for example. Gordon Ramsay Holdings finds a combination of organisational and individual-led mobility an effective strategy for developing talent.

Case study 1:

TALENT MOBILITY AT GORDON RAMSAY HOLDINGS

Initially employing 80 people, Gordon Ramsay Holdings (GRH) now has over 900 staff and has witnessed rapid expansion since its first restaurant – Restaurant Gordon Ramsay – opened in 1998. The organisation includes nine leading restaurants in London, consultancies in Dubai and Tokyo, new restaurants in Florida and New York, and there are plans to open more outlets in the USA and Europe in the future. The business is overseen by two chief executives, Gordon Ramsay and Chris Hutcheson (Gordon Ramsay's father-in-law). Gordon Ramsay plays a crucial role in the creative direction of the restaurants and works closely with the restaurant personnel, giving him the opportunity to identify talent in the restaurants and kitchens. This combined with his celebrity status has afforded the organisation a high-profile reputation within the hospitality and catering industry, both nationally and internationally.

Key drivers for talent management

Creative talent is key to the success of Gordon Ramsay Holdings. Gordon Ramsay, as one of the CEOs, places considerable importance on developing this talent within the organisation, which means that the business can continue to expand effectively throughout the UK and internationally. When opening a new restaurant, the organisation typically places a home-grown senior chef in charge of the new venture to work alongside senior restaurant staff taken from other restaurants in the business. Mark Sargeant, the head chef at Gordon Ramsay's at Claridges, for example, began working with Gordon Ramsay in 1998, and Marcus Wareing, the chef patron at Petrus, has worked with Gordon Ramsay for over ten years. Developing internal talent means that the organisation has also addressed recruitment difficulties associated with the lack of highly skilled chefs in the labour market.

Approaching talent management

Gordon Ramsay Holdings focuses its efforts on developing rather than recruiting talent, particularly in terms of the kitchen staff. Formal training is offered to employees (such as increasing staff knowledge of wines and cheese), but the talent-spotting and development of individuals is carried out by the line managers with the help of Gordon Ramsay.

Although restaurant staff and their ability to offer high standards of customer service are important for the business, talent is generally defined in terms of the creative cooking skills of the chefs. Because this creative talent plays an important role in the success of the business, not only in terms of expansion but also in terms of being publicly recognised through, for example, Michelin stars, a number of schemes operate to try to retain and develop these people.

Those chefs asked to head up a new restaurant are offered financial incentives to ensure that the new enterprise is successful. As part of their training, up-and-coming chefs are also sent on sabbaticals to improve their cooking skills. Typically, this involves working in a prestigious restaurant outside the UK for a lengthy period of time. These individuals are not obliged to return to Gordon Ramsay Holdings after they have finished their training – but invariably they do. As a head chef commented,

It's like your parents say – that if you love your children, you have to let them go.

On their return, the newly-trained chefs bring fresh ideas to the restaurant and also help to improve the skills of their colleagues. Gordon Ramsay explained how the sabbaticals worked:

[Having people leave your organisation and then come back] is a way of, I suppose, not just of getting a breath of fresh air, but enhancement. We're still growing, so we're nursing talent and losing talent, and having staff out there, like Neal, for the last 12 months, who's been on sabbatical, and I knew I had to do that to him before he opened New York. He couldn't come out of the Connaught and then go to New York and be highly successful. So what he's seen through Australia, what he's seen across South America, and Jason has seen a lot of places like Vietnam and Japan, you know, they come back with mind-boggling, extraordinary experiences and they're just bursting with enthusiasm to put it on a plate. So that sabbatical time-out is healthy and crucial.

How often would people get a sabbatical like this?

It depends, but it's always before a big opening [of a restaurant]. And that can vary between six and 12 months. That's not just life-changing but in terms of enhancement it's phenomenal, because it's just like the most amazing, exciting trip ever, and it's a one-off because you can't get into a serious partnership and then say 'I'm taking a year off' three years later.

So it's almost like a gap year?

Yeah. So we plan a year, 18 months in advance. When, for instance, Claridges was on and we were about to sign the lease – it would take a year to do in terms of re-vamp. I said to Mark – he was 27 – and I said, 'You know – play your cards right and in a year's time you're going to be chef de cuisine at Claridges.' He said, 'You know – I can't do that. I'm 27. I'm not even banqueting chef. He's 30, and he's not.' I said, 'Don't worry.' So they get that level of – not leg up – but a support mechanism. Which is crucial.

The benefits of internal development

For Gordon Ramsay Holdings, developing talent internally is a less risky and less costly approach to managing talent than recruiting it in. This approach means that they are able to expand successfully, retain talent within the business and guarantee that all staff are trained in 'the Gordon Ramsay way' to ensure continuity of service and standards. Retaining an informal, nurturing approach to managing talent has also enabled the organisation to remain creative – a key success factor in the competitive restaurant industry.

Gordon Ramsay Holdings' practice of sending talented chefs to develop their skills and experiences outside the organisation may seem radical but is reminiscent of the traditional approach taken to craft apprentices when they had completed their indentures and moved on to develop their expertise. The benefit to employers is a strengthening of the skills in the external talent pool.

Other case-study organisations are reviewing their approaches to mobility. For example, PricewaterhouseCoopers' Tim Richardson says that in doing some quite radical rethinking about how they support their graduate population in building their careers they have realised that, among other things,

This will involve moving people around more quickly so they obtain breadth of knowledge earlier... And the restrictions upon that are often in our own mindsets and traditions and the way we as individuals have done things for many, many years.

Mobility also involves individual choices and decisions. This is a factor which brings into focus the greater emphasis being placed in the employment relationship on individual ownership of personal learning and career development. Some of our interviewees on case-study talent management programmes did not necessarily see this as a negative trend.

Although there are the same opportunities for everyone, it is up to you what you do with it. The talent management programme allows a door to open, and it may close just as quickly, so it's up to you

to make it into something. It's like a LEGO box – you can create what you want: a tower or a bungalow ...

Participant on a talent management programme

STRETCH ASSIGNMENTS

Even if 'physical' mobility is not required, looking for opportunities to 'stretch' talented employees (eg through projects or deployment to a challenging role) is valuable. This reflects the CIPD's research into the shift from training to learning which highlights the benefits of 'on-the-job' learning as a 'self-directed, work-based process leading to increased adaptive capacity'.

Being prepared to give employees this kind of assignment is likely to mean organisations being required to take more of a risk – in order to aid the learning and development (and help the engagement and motivation) of talented individuals.

It is clear from this section that a number of issues must be considered in linking learning and development and talent management. Those we found to be most significant are listed in Table 9 below:

Diversity is a particular issue highlighted in the research – for example, the case of women managers. O'Neil and Bilimoria's (2005) women-only study looked at the career dynamics of women over their life course and the constraints on their talents of their 'non-traditional' work histories. They

Table 9 ❖ Managing the talent development process – some key questions	
Issue	Possible interventions
How can individuals be prepared for the next stage of development?	Those on talent programmes often learn by immersion in a completely different environment. Employees can be assigned to special projects in their own organisation or by taking a complete break to work in another organisation.
How can you address different rates in individual progress up the career ladder?	Recognise that slower progress up the career ladder does not necessarily mean that the candidate is not talented enough. Provide individualised career and development programmes. Ensure that you have good-quality conversations with your people to understand their motivations, preferences and priorities when it comes to career development – their aspirations may not match yours.
How would you advise those on talent management programmes about potential routes to progression and how to achieve it?	Consider having career progression support roles such as mentors or 'talent stewards' for those with high potential. These should be senior managers in the organisational 'know' politically or strategically who can help career development (but watch for potential problems where different mentors might be pushing different agendas).
How can you manage high-performing but plateaued staff who have reached their capability level?	Sabbaticals and secondments are a means of 're-energising' key employees who are high-performers but who do not have the potential for the talent pool. Other measures include training as mentors, sponsors and coaches.

recommend that better organisational efforts are needed to ensure that women receive on-going coaching and mentoring to build confidence, work for managers who support their development, and have access to organisational resources and tailored opportunities to develop their skills. At Standard Chartered PLC, for example, analysis was undertaken to highlight the numbers of women in each employment band and to address any issues of diversity in that area.

IMPLICATIONS FOR PRACTICE: TALENT MANAGEMENT AND LEARNING AND DEVELOPMENT

❖ *Appropriate learning and development interventions are required at relevant stages* in a career path for talented individuals to achieve their maximum potential. Developing talent needs informal as well as formal learning interventions.

❖ These interventions will include conventional development activities, *but there is also the opportunity to use creative alternatives such as talent coaching and mobility.*

❖ *Line managers, coaches and mentors should be adequately informed about the aims and objectives of a talent management initiative* and its links with corporate strategy.

❖ *Identify both internal and external development opportunities in order to 'stretch' participants* on a talent management programme to broaden their experiential learning.

❖ *Track individual career progression,* not least to ensure that there are appropriate development opportunities for talented employees at different stages of their careers.

❖ *Take individual employees' aspirations into account.* As one HR director noted: 'People are not chesspieces to be moved around the organisational chessboard.' Not every talented employee is seeking progression.

❖ *Pay attention to the part confidence plays in individuals' beliefs about their abilities and their self-selection* for talent management. In the case studies it was evident that this could be a particular barrier to entry for women, as suggested by other research on women's career progression.

MANAGING TALENT

7

- ❖ **How to link talent management to wider processes, such as performance management, is a key question being dealt with by employers.**

- ❖ **Employers place emphasis on the retention and internal development of talent as a strategic opportunity to make the best of the current workforce.**

- ❖ **Although staff turnover and retention of talent are viewed as important, organisations tend not to have a talent retention plan.**

- ❖ **Employee engagement is an important component of talent management and has significant implications for organisational practices, especially employee communications.**

MANAGING TALENT

Attracting talent and putting development programmes for talented individuals in place were identified as two parts of the talent management loop in an earlier chapter (see Figure 4 on page 19). The next arcs on the loop raised the question of how to manage talent and how to ensure that talented individuals stayed with the organisation after the investment in them. These were two further areas of research.

There was a good deal of emphasis on how exactly the management of talent, once identified, should take place.

> *Managing talent means being clear about what the different elements of the talent pipeline consist of, such as recruitment, selection, etc, and understanding which elements are more important at any particular time.*
>
> HR manager

> *When you are managing talent you have to be aware of where the pressure points are. Are we recruiting satisfactorily on the one hand, but losing people further down the pipeline at the same time?*
>
> HR manager

Managing talented individuals is of course a key part of any manager's job at all levels of the organisation. Our research focused on one aspect of this – linking talent management to the performance management process.

TALENT MANAGEMENT AND PERFORMANCE

Talent management has clear links with performance management, as revealed by the case-study organisations. What the research showed was that the approach to performance review – widely referred to as appraisal – was particularly important for those in the talent pool. This raises a number of questions:

- ❖ Should those in a talent pool be appraised differently or with greater frequency than those who are not, because of a need for closer monitoring of their performance in special high-profile projects?

- ❖ Should a formal performance review process play a large part in whether or not an employee is selected for a talent management programme?

- ❖ To what extent should managers be involved in the process of assessing potential as well as performance? (See also page 24 in Chapter 4.)

- ❖ Should there be set appraisal rating achievement for those in the pool where rating is in operation?

- ❖ How vital is the ongoing appraisal of the manager with regard to the management of talent?

Linking talent and performance management can be undertaken through the use of particular tools or a simple concept such as 'conversations that count', also used at

Appraisal is a key part of talent management at Standard Chartered, not only in its own right, but also because it is used to classify employees into five categories, ranging from high-potentials (HIPs) to underperformers. This system allows the Bank to manage its talent by revealing the skills and potential inside its workforce – and showing where there are gaps.

'HIPs are people with significant headroom, who would be expected to rise at least two further levels in the foreseeable future,' Haley (Group head of talent management and leadership development) explains. Second are critical resources: people who have the potential to improve and whom the Bank certainly wants to keep, but who are not real high-flyers. Third are core contributors. 'They are valuable resources who are probably doing what they do best now,' Haley says. Fourth are under-achievers, who could be doing better and should be helped to do so. Bottom of the pile are under-performers, who are 'in the wrong job and should be moved into another role or managed out'.

All employees, from juniors to one level below the board, are assessed annually according to this system in conjunction with their interim reviews. Combining classification with appraisal has kept the burden for managers to a minimum because they see it as part of the same process.

Source: Syedain (2007)

Standard Chartered PLC. Good-quality dialogue is a fundamental basis of effective talent management. Understanding and clarifying the roles of the players in this dialogue is an important part of the process. The following case study highlights an example of this.

Case study 8:

CONVERSATIONS THAT COUNT AT STANDARD CHARTERED PLC

Standard Chartered PLC is listed on both the London Stock Exchange and the Hong Kong Stock Exchange and is consistently ranked in the top 25 among FTSE-100 companies by market capitalisation. Standard Chartered has a history of over 150 years in banking and operates in many of the world's fastest-growing markets with an extensive global network of over 1,400 branches (including subsidiaries, associates and joint ventures) in over 50 countries in the Asia-Pacific Region, South Asia, the Middle East, Africa, the United Kingdom and the Americas.

As one of the world's most international banks, almost 60,000 people are employed, representing over 90 nationalities, worldwide. With strong organic growth supported by strategic alliances and acquisitions and driven by its strengths in the balance and diversity of its business, products, geography and people, Standard Chartered PLC is well positioned in the emerging trade corridors of Asia, Africa and the Middle East. The Bank derives over 90% of profits from Asia, Africa and the Middle East.

Key drivers for talent management

Standard Chartered PLC seeks to develop the capability to respond to market changes, evolve business strategies and achieve its ambitious growth aspirations, and these are the key drivers for its talent management initiatives. The HR function provides employee self-service and extensive data analysis across the Bank's 56 operating countries to allow all global HR processes to be consistently adopted and monitored across the Bank's markets.

The issues and challenges of talent management in Standard Chartered

The Bank is experiencing fast growth in the international domain, and it has a particular interest in ensuring that the talents of its diverse workforce are maximised through employee engagement and inclusivity. One way in which it is attempting to do this is through human capital management and the use of robust technologies. Data for all Standard Chartered PLC's direct employees across 56 markets are held on one HR management information system, Peoplewise, which is powered by Peoplesoft technology. Using comparable, standardised and robust data provided through the global Peoplesoft system and the Human Resources Shared Service Centre in Chennai, India, the Bank is able to provide extensive data reporting capability. This strategy enables most of its global processes to be consistently tracked across the Bank's markets, including data on core demographics, performance, reward, training, talent management, diversity, and development progress. It also helps to ensure management accountability and therefore accuracy of data.

'Conversations that count'

Alignment of different aspects of talent management is another challenge, and SCB have a number of initiatives that seek to address it. One particularly successful example is through the use of five briefings entitled *Conversations that Count*, which are short guides to quickly enable managers to have vital conversations with each member of their teams. Conversations on performance and on development have a set schedule that involves planning in January, reviewing in July, and assessing in December.

These five main 'conversations' take place on a flexible basis on engagement, strengths and career, and are related to the needs of the individual team member. It is felt that when a conversation between manager and employee is the 'right' conversation undertaken in the 'right' way, it can help increase engagement, enable people to develop and use their strengths, enable the Bank to keep its best talent, encourage energy, innovation and fun, satisfy customers, and deliver better business and financial results.

Managers are advised that their HR regional manager can then help them access further sources of support if needed, including training programmes and extra information on their HR information system. These conversations are:

Perform

At the start of January employees are asked to draft business and financial objectives for the year ahead and consider how they will deliver the values of the business during the year. A meeting is then arranged to discuss this, and managers will also share information that provides context – eg their own objectives. SMART objectives are then agreed and consideration given to what the objectives mean for the employee's learning.

Learn and develop

At the start of January the employee is asked to draft a document that will set out: what he or she needs to learn – bearing in mind objectives and future career goals, and how he or she needs to learn – drawing on a wide range of learning options. A meeting is held with the manager to discuss the learning the employee needs in order to achieve excellence in the role and deliver this year's objectives. Resource constraints such as time and budget have to be considered and how to work imaginatively within those constraints. The year's learning and development priorities are then agreed, written down and signed off.

Build careers

The time may be right for a career conversation when the employee has mastered the core aspects of his or her job and is ready for additional or fresh challenges and it has been 12–18 months since the last career conversation. A meeting takes place where the employee discusses his or her career goals. Tools are provided beforehand to assist with the employee's reflections.

Engagement review

A 'lite' engagement review takes place once a year with existing team members already known well by the manager. Ahead of the meeting the individual is briefed, open questions are asked during the meeting, and agreed actions recorded and commitment made to follow up. A 'full' engagement review is for team members who are new to the manager. During the meeting, the manager is required to ask open, focused questions under the headings: 'Know me', 'Care about me' and 'Focus on me'.

Build strengths

In order to have the 'great conversation', when the manager and the HR manager believe the time is right, the employee is asked to complete an online questionnaire called StrengthsFinder™ which is designed to identify talents and strengths. It need only be completed once because the talents it reveals are enduring; it is used to support the development of a person who performs well and has high potential. One of the Bank's Strengths coaches helps the employee to understand the talents it reveals, and how he or she can be developed towards strengths. The conversation with the manager takes place after this to explore what the employee has learned, to discuss the actions he or she will take to develop talents into strengths, to consider opportunities to use his or her talents and strengths more often, and to record agreed actions and sign off. The employee is encouraged to have a follow-up session with the Strengths coach every six months.

So 'Conversations that count' are an essential way in which different elements of talent management are aligned.

Standard Chartered PLC's approach is a highly structured and integrated one involving steps that make the process clear to the managers undertaking the reviews by focusing on the dialogue that is required to take place in various conversations. This notion of 'conversation' also appears in other areas of HR practices which relate to talent management. For example, Hirsh (2003, p.237) suggests that the succession planning process also involves dialogue between key parties, and she coins the useful term 'succession dialogues'.

TALENT MANAGEMENT AND REWARD

The research did not specifically explore reward, but a number of issues arose in terms of the impact reward systems could have on talent management initiatives, particularly in terms of retaining talent. This is an area that can only be touched on in this report but it is clearly an area in need of further investigation. To appreciate the dominance of rewards in people management strategies, it is worth noting the following key findings of a study carried out by Innecto Reward Consulting (2006):

❖ Cultural, economic and technological changes in the past 10 years have made financial reward a greater motivator than challenging work or personal pride.

❖ Nearly three-quarters of the 690 'career-oriented' UK executives under 40 years old who were polled said they now expected a pay rise every year.

❖ Two-thirds claimed that financial reward is now the number one career motivator.

❖ Yet just 15% of the 189 HR professionals surveyed believed financial reward to be a key motivator.

These findings suggest that unless there is a joined-up approach to rewards and talent management, an investment in talent management activities may just not be worthwhile – but it also indicates that HR must be far more alert to the problem – particularly as 75% of those surveyed admitted that their businesses had lost at least five talented staff in 2005. The following observation illustrates the complex issues that can arise in the relationship between compensation practice and talent management, especially in an international context.

In this organisation compensation is increasingly being related to both the performance and the potential of the employee in addition, as all businesses will be required to have a people strategy and the compensation strategy will be an essential component in this.

However, because we have decided to focus on external competitiveness as opposed to internal equity, in our compensation practices in the

respective business units sometimes we have problems in creating development opportunities for some of our employees. [For] example, if we want to move an employee from a Business A [that has a very aggressive pay practice according to the industry] to the Business B [that has a more conservative pay practice], it will be a challenge because we cannot change the approach to compensation of Business B to meet the employee from Business A.

International HR director

Reward is clearly a major area for attention at the design stage of talent management strategy. Unless it is taken into account, increasing investment in talent management does little to retain key individuals.

TALENT MANAGEMENT AND RETENTION

Our research, then, highlighted how talented individuals were retained within the organisation.

The 2006 CIPD Recruitment, Retention and Turnover survey found that although employers' ability to retain employees generally continues to improve, the retention of talent was still a key issue. The survey reported that 69% of respondents experienced retention difficulties, a fall from 73% in 2004 and 77% in 2003. It therefore found little evidence of any long-term trend towards higher staff turnover. The report also included a number of other significant findings, listed in the box opposite.

Retention is a significant part of talent management and the figures in the box opposite suggest that job tenure is currently stable. But one talent management survey reports that nearly 68% of respondents do not have a talent retention plan. The picture is worse in the public sector, over 80% of public sector organisations indicating they have no real plans for talent retention even though significant problems are also reported in retaining specialist workers (SOCPO, 2005, p.4–5). So whereas the general picture on staff turnover may be improving, it seems that this is not the result of targeted plans for retaining talent.

One possible explanation for a lack of attention to plans for retaining talent is that it is possible to sustain high-quality service provision despite having a high staff turnover rate.

In talent management high turnover can be both an advantage and a disadvantage to the organisation. The points that are applicable to talent management probably reflect employee turnover in its wider sense (see Table 10 opposite).

These pros and cons of employee turnover operate differently in different organisations and at different points in time. In general, though, and in talent management in particular, low staff turnover is desirable.

FINDINGS OF THE CIPD RECRUITMENT, RETENTION AND TURNOVER SURVEY 2006

❖ Overall employee turnover rate for the UK is 18.3%.

❖ A third of employees in the UK have been in their current jobs for over ten years, while 10% have stayed for over 20 years. Average job tenure has remained remarkably stable over the last 30 years, falling among men but rising among women.

❖ Turnover levels vary considerably from industry to industry.

❖ The highest levels of turnover (22.9%) are found in private sector organisations.

❖ The highest levels (commonly in excess of 50% per annum) are found in retailing, hotels and restaurants, call centres and among other lower-paid private sector services groups.

❖ The public sector has an average turnover rate of 13.3%. Turnover levels also vary from region to region.

❖ The highest rates are found where unemployment is lowest and where it is unproblematic for people to secure desirable alternative employment.

Interventions such as role-modelling enables an organisation to build a reputation and culture that shows it is the kind of place where replicating these behaviours can prepare employees for filling key leadership and top management positions in the future. In turn, this can build up reservoirs of talent within the organisation.

Standard Chartered PLC reports that it links leadership with role-modelling. One way it does this is by bringing together 'Emerging Leaders' to listen to senior and executive staff telling stories about their experiences in challenging business and personal situations. It also makes links between diversity and

role-modelling by bringing internal female senior talent to talk to high-potential staff. For example, women's lunches are held at which female senior managers share their experiences of working at senior level in different geographies, such as Pakistan and Hong Kong.

Such activities make clear to identified talent both what is expected and required to fill senior roles, and helps to develop the desired characteristics and behaviours. This increases the probability that identified talent remains with the Bank and that the Bank in turn can fill senior vacancies. These activities do not, however, guarantee that talented employees are retained.

Table 10 ❖ The pros and cons of employee turnover	
Pros	Cons
Turnover can be beneficial where:	Turnover can cause problems where:
❖ poor performers leaving can be replaced by more effective employees	❖ lost skills are relatively scarce
❖ replacing employees with outmoded thinking or talents with those with innovative ideas and skills and knowledge more appropriate to current requirements	❖ recruitment costs of replacements is high
	❖ it takes longer time-scales to fill vacancies
❖ it can enable a review of future business staffing requirements and change in job and personnel specification to reflect new talent needs	❖ customers value relationships with those individual employees who have left
	❖ talent leaves to join direct competitors
	❖ high turnover includes a high proportion of talented employees

The CIPD 2006 Recruitment, Retention and Turnover survey reported that the most popular actions taken by organisations to address general retention are:

❖ improving the induction process (49%)

❖ offering increased learning and development opportunities (45%), and

❖ improved selection techniques (38%).

Induction and selection are not specifically mentioned in our case studies. The benefits provided in our cases to aid retention of talent included:

❖ faster progression up the career ladder

❖ flexible working, and

❖ management/leadership development programmes.

An additional way to retain employees is to obtain a level of fit between an organisation's values and those of the employee (Edwards, 2005). This can be achieved at the recruitment stage, by appointing staff with similar values to those of the organisation, and also through focused training and development and performance management.

Coaching is particularly valued by our senior-level respondents. As a customised development process, coaching enables identification and development of individual potential and can help increase performance as well as retention.

TALENT LEAVING THE ORGANISATION

The CIPD Recruitment, Retention and Turnover survey (2006) found that employees resign for many different reasons.

❖ Pull factors include the attraction of a new job or the prospect of a period outside the workforce.

❖ Push factors include dissatisfaction with a present job or circumstances outside the control of any employer, such as relocation of a partner.

There are strong suggestions that push factors are a great deal more significant in most resignations and it is relatively rare for people to leave jobs in which they are happy, even when offered higher pay elsewhere.

Talent management programmes can sometimes have unanticipated effects, such as 'pushing' core employees to take their (often expensively) developed skills elsewhere. The risk of losing highly developed employees is one that must be expected but not ignored. It can also have positive benefits – as suggested by one manager at PricewaterhouseCoopers:

We recruit and train so many good financial specialists that when they go elsewhere, it is to the benefit of the profession as a whole.

In our research some employees were surprised (but pleased) at their employer's willingness to take the risk that they might leave. One commented that

They are quite open about that. There is no commitment to stay with the organisation if you go on the talent management programme.

Another said,

It's a brave, high-risk strategy. The talent management people become more employable so they may leave.

It is important that investment in learning and development as part of talent management programmes provides a return. It is equally important, therefore, that most talent is retained.

GETTING A BALANCE IN TURNOVER

As indicated above, talent management can have unforeseen and unintended consequences. Employees become not only more employable but also begin to think about how their talents might be welcome elsewhere, perhaps in a more challenging role or where the rewards are greater. This indicates a direct connection between talent management and a focus on staff turnover.

It is important to get the balance right with staff turnover since organisations need both 'new blood' and retention of key talent. However, based on our research, few organisations seem to take account of talent leaving the organisation. There are nonetheless positive steps that can be taken.

❖ Maintain contact with leavers, especially in the first month when they might feel they have made the wrong decision.

❖ Do not discourage employees to work outside the organisation, but encourage them to return.

❖ Use sabbaticals to refresh commitment and provide new experiences.

❖ Establish an employee alumni association and encourage contact to be maintained.

In one organisation we visited, the use of an alumni association has resulted in several valued employees returning to the organisation.

What is always important is that employees contribute to their full potential while employed. Employee engagement helps to achieve this, as well as contributing to retention and talent management more widely.

EMPLOYEE ENGAGEMENT

Employee engagement has been defined as 'the willingness and ability to contribute to the organisation's success' (Towers Perrin, 2004, p.12) or, as in the CIPD report *Working Life: Employee attitudes and engagement*, it is viewed more simply as 'passion for work' (Truss *et al*, 2006, p.2). The aspects of a job that attract people are quite different from those aspects that keep people and those that engage them to give discretionary effort on the job. According to this recent research, an interconnected set of emotional, cognitive and physical dimensions together construct the psychological state termed 'employee engagement'. This psychological state reflects emotional attachment to the job and work, a strong intellectual focus on the job while at work and a willingness to 'go the extra mile' for the organisation. The key factors driving engagement are:

❖ opportunities to feed views upwards

❖ feeling well-informed about the organisation

❖ the belief that managers are committed to the organisation.

Among our case organisations, Google illustrates well the importance and benefits of employee engagement.

Case study 9:

EMPLOYEE ENGAGEMENT AT GOOGLE

Founded in 1998 by Stanford PhD students Larry Page and Sergey Brin, Google's mission is simple – to organise the world's information and make it universally accessible and useful. This core belief, in democratising access to information, has led Google into new areas of innovation and also investment in countries around the world, as Google products are localised to local needs. Google is now truly international, with a significant portion of traffic to google.com coming from outside the United States, in addition to the traffic to local sites in each country.

Approaching talent management

Because Google operates in a fluid working environment, talent management is delivered through a balance of formal and more flexible systems. Performance is measured against goals set out each quarter, yet managers and HR specialists also nurture talent throughout someone's career. More recently, Google has introduced a limited number of fast-track programmes to encourage the promotion of talent internally.

Of course, talent management can only start with hiring the right people. Google devotes a considerable amount of resource to this, with great success. Appointing staff who are not only skilled but able to think 'outside the box' and creatively is a key priority for the company. Recruiting exceptionally skilled staff does not present difficulties for Google because of the way in which Google allows people with talent to develop and grow according to their own skills and opportunities that present themselves.

Issues and challenges

The average age of the Google workforce in Dublin is 24. Many employees are highly talented graduates and for numerous staff this is their first job after leaving education. One HR director summarised this workforce profile by describing Google as 'like a university campus'. Staff are encouraged to challenge the status quo in their jobs, which means that the workforce have high expectations of Google as an employer. For line managers, managing these demands can be a challenge because there is great pressure to keep these people interested and motivated. As one European sales director commented,

We ... purposefully go out of our way to hire very intelligent people, and that creates a very challenging management environment because you need to keep these people interested.

Google has introduced various financial and non-financial rewards to help tackle this tension. Spot-bonuses are available for great work and employees share in the success of the company through a company plan and option scheme.

Google also has a number of non-financial benefits available to all staff, such as free food, new offices, free entertainment which supplements their salary, in addition to global job opportunities. Many employees also get the chance to design their own working environment. As one HR specialist said:

This is the thing that keeps them here ... They can pick their own job titles, they can pick their coffee machines, they can just do anything they want ...

Another benefit is that the Dublin office has so many different nationalities working in the team, alongside the native Dubliners: 42 countries are represented in the 1,000 staff. Furthermore, in some teams overseas staff may eventually return home. This does not always mean that the staff leave Google, though, because where possible they are placed in Google offices in their home country.

Benefits so far

Although Google's approach to talent management is not typical of more bureaucratic organisations, it is still able to recruit and retain highly talented staff. This has enabled it to remain innovative in the marketplace. Of course, Google is always looking at new ways to both recruit and develop its talent, through a mix of formal and informal measures. As Google invests further, more formalised measures may be appropriate and Google will continue to evaluate the best way it can do this.

IMPLICATIONS FOR PRACTICE – MANAGING AND RETAINING TALENT

This chapter has looked at some of the research findings for managing and retaining talent, and from these it is possible to highlight some of the key implications:

❖ *Develop a performance culture* where individuals take responsibility for the continuous improvement of business processes and their own skills development.

❖ *The performance expectations of individuals in talent pools must be carefully defined* and communicated. Managers undertaking their performance reviews are central in this process.

❖ *Ensure that good-quality conversations* take place between individuals and managers regarding their performance, development needs, motivation and aspirations in the organisation.

❖ *Train managers in having 'the difficult conversation'* when managing the performance of those on formal talent programmes and those that have not been selected.

❖ *Be sensitive to the impact of reward systems on talented individuals* and make sure there is a joined-up approach to rewards and talent management.

❖ *Active steps, plans and activities are needed to retain and engage talent* which is required for the future health of the organisation.

❖ *Investment in management, leadership and other development activities* will positively impact on talent retention.

❖ *Clear career development paths* and swift, rather than slow, progression will positively impact on retention.

❖ *Employee engagement can be an important concept* and component of retention strategies within overall talent management programmes. Open communications with opportunities for upward feedback will positively impact on engagement, as will demonstrated commitment to the organisation from managers.

❖ *Role-modelling* will positively impact on retention.

❖ *Some level of staff turnover is healthy and beneficial.* Talent that leaves, though, should not be forgotten, and contact can and should be maintained.

WHO MAKES TALENT MANAGEMENT HAPPEN? 8

❖ **Successful talent management depends on the combined contributions of the Chief Executive, the board, senior management, HR and talent management specialists, line managers and employees themselves.**

❖ **It relies on a shared organisational understanding of their respective roles and responsibilities.**

❖ **Line managers play a pivotal role in developing talented individuals.**

❖ **A coaching culture with trained coaches is a key ingredient in developing organisational talent.**

INTRODUCTION

The report has noted that a critical success factor in talent management initiatives is a shared understanding of what is meant by talent and talent management within an organisation. The next, equally critical, stage is making sure that the CEO, the board, senior management, HR and talent management specialists, line managers and employees are aware of their respective roles and responsibilities in making talent management happen.

Interviews conducted as part of the research revealed that it is important not only to clarify the roles of individuals but to pay proper attention to gaining their commitment to any talent management initiatives. Their engagement depends on how well the aims and detail of any talent management interventions are communicated and, in the case of line managers, the extent of their early involvement. But our interviewees saw the most important factor in gaining engagement at all levels of the organisation as top-down support from the outset of any talent management programme.

SUPPORT FROM THE TOP

> Talent management has to be communicated as a strategic priority and visibly supported by the most senior levels of management to maximise employee engagement with its aims and processes.

The key role marked out in the case-study organisations for senior management is their visible involvement in the formulating of a talent management initiative and the communicating of it to the workforce. HR professionals report that senior management commitment is the essential ingredient in how it is then viewed by the workforce, and the importance attached to it.

The focus groups confirmed that participants placed more value on talent management programmes if they saw that they were supported at the highest level of the organisation. The presence of executive team members at talent management launches and other development events was cited as evidence of organisational commitment by those in the identified talent pool.

When directors came along to our final presentations on the Leading Manager programme, it really was encouraging to know there was interest at the very top in what we were saying ... It did increase my commitment.

The executive directors have sponsored the programme ... They have shown lots of commitment and really engaged with it – they attended the first event, so you really can't ask more than that.

Where senior managers also acted as coaches to individuals or had a recognised mentoring role, it was reported by our talent management participants to offer particular benefits in terms of providing organisational opportunities. As this talent programme participant observed:

Having a member of the executive as my coach has really opened doors for me... It has made me known, whereas before it would have been the same old faces on the project I am working on.

Several of the case-study organisations have talent panels which include senior management representatives. This was the case at PricewaterhouseCoopers LLP, the Legal Services Commission, Standard Chartered PLC and Cargill. The responsibilities of such panels varied, but frequently included:

❖ the initial design of talent management initiatives

❖ selecting individuals for the talent pool

❖ reviewing the progress of talent management activities against identified strategic objectives

❖ identifying areas for attention – for example, recruitment and retention issues or line management support

❖ addressing mobility issues and the progression of talented individuals across the organisation

❖ mentoring and coaching high-potential individuals.

THE CONTRIBUTION OF THE HR FUNCTION

The research suggests that the HR function's main contribution is largely perceived to be a support role in the design and application of talent management interventions. But we found considerable variation between the case-study organisations in the extent to which HR specialists are a source of proactivity in their support and guidance. Despite talent management's acknowledged support role, the responsibility for developing talent management policies was very clearly identified as falling in the domain of the HR function.

At PricewaterhouseCoopers LLP and Standard Chartered PLC there are designated talent management/human capital specialists responsible for designing and supporting talent management strategies and practices. They have a specific responsibility for ensuring that each element of the talent pipeline is given equal attention and that clear guidance is communicated to the different stakeholders in the process.

In contrast, at Google the input from HR is informal. Although Gordon Ramsay Holdings has no formal talent management activities, at a 'local' level chefs and restaurant managers are supported in decisions on talent management by the HR function. The HR function at the Legal Services Commission has provided a comprehensive internal consultancy service in the development and implementation of its talent management programme, as illustrated in the box below:

THE LSC'S INTERNAL CONSULTANCY SERVICE

The design of the talent management programme at the Legal Services Commission has been informed by research undertaken by a member of the HR team who acts as the consultant for the talent management programme. The HR director felt strongly from the outset that talent management should not be managed by the HR function but be led by the directors of the organisation.

The talent management initiative began with a group of some 16 stakeholders, selected to represent a reasonable cross-section of the organisation and supported by an external consultant from Roffey Park. This team met for two days each month for six months to work on an organisational definition of talent management and design a scheme to meet the strategic aim of developing internal talent for the future leadership of the organisation.

To ensure a continuing engagement of the organisation's senior management, the project group's recommendation was to establish a talent panel with as much representation from the six directors of the organisation as possible.

In deciding on the approach that would best suit the needs of the Commission, the internal HR consultant explored talent management approaches in other organisations. This investigation led to a focus on the individual ownership of personal development, which is a defining characteristic of the Commission's programme. The initial research work undertaken by HR has paid dividends.

Members of the talent pool reported that their confidence in the scheme increased when they learned of the thorough evaluation undertaken by HR of alternative approaches. It was felt this demonstrated that time had been invested in designing a scheme that best fitted the needs of the organisation and those of high-potential individuals. This is evident in the comment of this talent programme participant:

My belief in the scheme really grew when I learnt of all the work that had been done by HR into approaches in other organisations resulting in a programme being developed that was designed to meet our needs.

TALENT MANAGEMENT AND LINE MANAGERS

In common with Hutchinson and Purcell's (2003) conclusion that line managers play the pivotal role in people management, our study reveals the vital part line management plays in the implementation of talent management. Where such responsibilities are viewed by line managers as an important and integral part of their role, it is most likely to be in an operational environment where:

❖ there is established effective partnership working between line management and the HR function in the design and application of HR policies

❖ personal development planning is shared by the individual and his or her line manager as an integral part of a performance review process.

The major vehicle for line managers to spot individual talent is the performance review process. In all the case-study organisations, performance review had a developmental focus as well as, in most instances, an evaluation of past performance.

> Direct line managers are the key enabler or a constraint on developing individual talent and the main gatekeepers for accessing organisational opportunities.

In common with the trend in recent years, the majority of our case-study organisations have increased the level of HR responsibilities devolved to line management, their role in performance appraisal being a cornerstone of those responsibilities. We found that, in practice, there are concerns about the resultant heavy reliance on line management as talent-spotters and the nurturers of potential. This could lead to very different individual experiences, as suggested by these interviewees:

> It all depends on the level of interest shown by your line manager. I am very lucky – my line manager is a people person and has really helped to develop me – but not everyone has the same experience. It really is the luck of the draw.

> We do discuss my development but the service demands are ever-increasing and I can see that if I was to develop through working on corporate projects it would be a problem for my line manager in getting a replacement for me.

As this last observation illustrates, a dilemma for line managers in nurturing employee potential is that there may be adverse consequences for them in doing so if the end result is the loss of a talented individual. This was an issue acknowledged by line managers, HR specialists and employees alike. Where resources are particularly constrained but meeting performance targets is a key priority, some of our interviewees suggested that a line manager could actually represent a barrier to a possible secondment, a promotion or even the release of an individual to attend a development programme.

Although the conflicting objectives managers could face are recognised and understood, our research suggests that a consistent and corporate approach is needed to ensure that high-potential employees are equitably treated. This is where the presence of a talent panel pays dividends by providing a wider organisational overview.

A more complex issue to resolve is the suggestion by some respondents that an individual in the identified talent pool could be regarded as a possible threat by his or her line manager, particularly if such an employee had readier access to or more regular contact with senior people than the line manager. There was a reported concern about the application of the usual performance processes in these instances by the direct line manager. It was a situation that became more difficult when an individual in the talent pool had been seconded, for example, to work on a special project but the reporting lines remained unchanged.

> It is important to have an early involvement of line management in talent programmes to address any concerns they may have, to communicate the contribution they are expected to make, and to provide supportive training.

Senior managers and HR specialists in some of the case-study organisations recognised that engaging the line managers is an area in which more work should be done; this emerged as a strong theme in the public sector organisations, as evident in the comments of two HR directors:

> We do expect a significant involvement from the line manager ... That is one of the things the talent panel monitors, but we know we have more to do to get them fully on board ... We are looking at how we can do this for the next cohort.

> This is a large and complex organisation and we are heavily dependent on line managers identifying potential. The reality is that the employee experience is likely to be patchy, which is one of the reasons why we need to ensure a consistent approach to personal development as part of our Achievement and Development process.

In those organisations where there is a reliance on informal processes, recognising individual talent may be viewed as even more of a lottery, as the following employee observations reveal.

It all depends on your line manager. Those who shout loudest tend to get heard – but I must say I have had great support from my own line managers.

As far as my own talent management is concerned, I feel I can have a two-way conversation on my career and development needs with my manager – absolutely.

It's really up to your line manager whether you get the opportunities you need to develop yourself. Harnessing and developing talent is down to the personality of individual managers.

As already mentioned, our findings reveal the centrality of the appraisal process in engaging line managers in talent management as part of their responsibilities for the development and performance of their staff. Where this requires a formal process of personal development planning, there is:

❖ a wider awareness among managers of their responsibilities for developing individuals and monitoring their progress

❖ a greater likelihood that talent management activities are integrated with existing performance and development processes.

> The presence of a universally applied, understood and respected performance review is seen as the key means of reducing inconsistency of treatment and variations in employees' experiences.

In those case-study organisations with a culture of mentoring and coaching, managers were found to be more conscious of the contribution they could make in identifying and developing talented individuals. This was informed not only by their experience of coaching someone in the organisation but also by their own personal experience of being coached, usually by a more senior manager.

To sum up: our data suggests that although line managers are supportive of the principle of identifying and nurturing individual talent, as a group they are aware of a number of concerns arising from their managerial responsibilities for individuals beyond those in the identified talent pool. These are set out in the box below.

Before we consider the responsibilities of individual employees in talent management activities, it is worth considering some of the concerns we heard them expressing (see opposite). Some of these mirror those identified by line managers summarised in the box below.

SEVEN CONCERNS MOST FREQUENTLY MENTIONED BY LINE MANAGERS ABOUT TALENT MANAGEMENT

1 Line managers feel they should be part of the process of selecting candidates for talent management programmes, particularly in terms of endorsing individuals.

2 Talent management programmes may provide excellent development programmes or secondments but there are concerns that some individuals in key roles could be penalised where it is difficult to release them.

3 There may be a difficulty in knowing how to deal with demotivated employees not recognised as part of the talent pool after undergoing a formal selection process.

4 Providing development for participants on a talent programme should not be at the cost of development for the majority and investing in broader management training.

5 There is potential conflict between managing individual expectations about promotion prospects and the realism of accelerated progression within an organisational context of flatter structures and a tradition of long service in key roles.

6 That individuals may have been labelled as organisational talent could prove problematic in terms of managing day-to-day performance issues and involve a perceived loss of managerial control if they are working on projects outside the span of a line manager's area of responsibility.

7 There must be clarity on how talent management initiatives are to be operated alongside other HR policies – for example, training and development programmes, geographical mobility requirements or open-access recruitment designed to provide equality of opportunity.

SEVEN CONCERNS MOST FREQUENTLY MENTIONED BY EMPLOYEES ABOUT TALENT MANAGEMENT

1 Not feeling it is appropriate to apply for a talent management programme due to a recent promotion or being in a key role and recognising the problems of replacement

2 Concern about the potential for divisiveness if some individuals are labelled as 'talented' and others not, and the lack of transparency where an individual is in the talent pool but it is not made known to colleagues

3 A lack of geographical mobility that prevents career progression and reduces the chances of being identified in the talent pool if not working in the corporate head office

4 Limited opportunities for progression despite being on the talent management programme; whether those in the talent pool would be considered for opportunities in the first instance

5 An absence of talent management programmes for technical specialists who are not pursuing a general management route to progression

6 More resources for development going to a select few, reducing the resources available to the wider workforce

7 Issues of diversity in the talent pool in terms of older workers or employees not working full-time.

THE RESPONSIBILITIES OF INDIVIDUALS

The research found that the requirement to produce a personal development plan was the main means of encouraging individual ownership for self-development. The degree of responsibility for personal development expected of individuals varied across the case-study organisations, although in some instances it was an integral part of the performance review process. The extent to which individuals took the initiative for developing themselves was singled out for comment by managers, HR specialists and some participants on talent management programmes.

In some instances it was felt that individuals were accustomed to taking a passive role towards development opportunities, and that this was a culture that ought to change.

> There has been a tradition of individuals seeing development as something that is 'done to them' by attending courses. In my view we need to get away from that perception by encouraging individuals to actively seek out opportunities to grow themselves and to be responsible for managing their own learning.

HR director

In one of the case-study organisations, the recently introduced talent management programme places a heavy emphasis on participants owning their personal development and identifying what they need to focus on based on their personal development plan. The progress individuals are making is monitored by the talent management panel who meet quarterly with the scheme's participants. There are also meetings with individual executive mentors responsible for assisting with development opportunities to meet the needs of individuals, but the expectation is that participants will seek out development opportunities:

> You do have to identify opportunities for your development against your personal plan and go knocking on doors ... It was slow going to start with, and it took some time to realise what I had to do, but now it is really working well ... This tailored approach really suits me.

Talent programme participant

This approach is highly tailored to each participant's requirements but is also one that places a considerable onus on the participants in the programme to be proactive in developing themselves. Certain individuals found this more challenging than others, but the small numbers involved in the current programme made it easier to support those involved. There was a general recognition that as the programme is extended to all grades in the organisation, there will have to be a rather more structured approach than at the present time.

Employees in the focus groups reported that being selected for the talent programme had increased their sense of responsibility for maximising the investment that was being made in them – as this observation from one individual illustrates:

It could be seen as a high-risk strategy, making so much of an investment in just a few individuals, but it does make you realise you need to make the very most of the opportunities being given to you.

USING COACHES AND MENTORS

Although already considered earlier, it would be remiss not to draw attention to the part played by those individuals who act as coaches and mentors to individuals in the talent pool within some of our case-study organisations. As Hutchinson and Purcell (2007) report in the CIPD Change Agenda on the role of line managers in training, learning and development, the pastoral role of line managers as mentors and coaches should not be underestimated. Our research reveals that where there has been an investment in developing coaching skills, particularly among managers, it provides a crucial means of support for talent management initiatives.

The roles that our research reveals are most frequently identified with the different parties in talent management interventions are summarised in Table 11 below.

IMPLICATIONS FOR PRACTICE

❖ *The roles and responsibilities of different stakeholders* in talent management activities should be carefully identified at the design and development stage.

❖ *The CEO and senior management must be visible* in terms of leading talent management strategy development and in its implementation.

❖ *HR specialists have a key role in supporting the design and delivery of talent management strategy and practice* to meet the future resourcing requirements of the organisation by:

    ❖ researching alternative approaches and evaluating their organisational appropriateness

    ❖ making sure that processes are in place and that they happen

    ❖ managing the information flow and communicating details of talent management activities

Table 11 ❖ The contributions of different parties to talent management

CEO and senior management	❖ Strategy development ❖ Communicating the aims of talent management ❖ Selecting the talent pool ❖ Visible support for talent management interventions ❖ Representation on the talent management panel ❖ Executive coaches and mentors
Human resource and talent management specialists	❖ Researching and evaluating alternative approaches ❖ Advice and support with the design and implementation process ❖ Information flow about TM activities ❖ Monitoring TM interventions ❖ Tracking the progress of the TM pool ❖ Support for the TM panel
Line management	❖ Identifying talent ❖ Nurturing talent ❖ Performance review and individual personal development planning ❖ Facilitating the development of high-potential individuals ❖ Monitoring and tracking their progress ❖ Coaching and mentoring
Individuals	❖ Ownership of personal development ❖ Proactive approach to personal development planning ❖ Maximising learning opportunities
Talent management panel	❖ Senior management presence but representatives from across the organisation ❖ Monitoring and evaluating strategic outcomes ❖ Organisational overview and consistency of approach ❖ Tracking the progression of the talent pool ❖ Reviewing and amending initiatives

TALENT: STRATEGY, MANAGEMENT, MEASUREMENT

- ❖ providing impartial advice and support for the different stakeholders, such as talent panels, line managers, coaches, those in talent pools and individual employees

- ❖ ensuring that talent management activities are integrated with other HR policies

- ❖ monitoring programmes and identifying issues to be addressed.

❖ *It is important to have an early engagement of line management* in talent programmes, with a proper clarification of the contribution they are expected to make and supportive training.

❖ *An accountable talent management review panel* with senior management representatives can be an effective way of auditing, implementing and ensuring that talent is strategically and consistently developed across the organisation.

❖ *Individual employees within the organisation must be encouraged to actively seek out opportunities* to manage their own learning and take responsibility for developing their own careers.

❖ *A supportive organisational culture* for talent management activities is created by developing mentors and trained coaches across the organisation.

TRACKING AND EVALUATING TALENT MANAGEMENT

9

❖ **Quantitative approaches to the evaluation of talent management are not commonly applied.**

❖ **Systems for tracking and monitoring talent are similarly not widely utilised.**

❖ **Evaluation of talent management is difficult but necessary to ensure that the investment in talent management is meeting organisational needs.**

❖ **Evaluation requires both quantitative and qualitative data which is valid, reliable and robust.**

INTRODUCTION

There is a growing requirement for HR professionals to demonstrate measurement of their activities – to show returns on investment in HR and to show progress against key initiatives. Our research investigated how this had been applied to talent management.

The case was well put by the HR specialists at Google, who reported that the high speed of organisational growth required equally speedy responses to recruiting, deploying and developing talent and the necessity of joining up different elements of the pipeline to ensure ease of progress of individuals through the career structure. Both these demand good information (although some talent data is less easy to identify than others, such as turning creativity into metrics). Such information can be tactical – tracking measures, for example – or strategic as part of human capital management.

The requirement for good information was highlighted in a previous report, *Talent Management: Understanding the dimensions* (CIPD, 2006), which noted the fact that to undertake successful talent management it is necessary to track progress of identified talent against agreed success criteria. To do this requires an organisation-wide talent information management system and associated technology.

However, our research revealed that the majority of cases do little in terms of monitoring to evaluate the success of any talent management process. This finding supports the 2004 WERS finding (Kersley *et al*, 2006) that monitoring by the HR function is an underdeveloped activity even though HR specialists recognise that it is important to gain an informed corporate picture of how effectively talent is being developed. Issues of confidentiality and a fragmented approach to

performance appraisal contribute to the frequently reported absence of sufficiently detailed knowledge of what is taking place at operational level.

However, where measures are undertaken, they have proved to add value to the talent management proceess. Areas being examined included:

❖ the numbers and sources of employees included in the talent management process

❖ the alignment of measures of talent at each point in the talent 'pipeline' to key performance indicators (KPIs) supports the collection of large amounts of data

❖ the number of talented people aimed for in a particular organisational context. Figures mentioned in discussions were that only 2% to 3% of 'rising stars' might usefully be identified for high-potential programmes. This does, though, depend on the size of a particular organisation. In Cargill, for example, 3% is a large number, but for others it will represent only double figures. It is therefore crucial to set out initially in the evaluation and tracking processes the proportion and absolute numbers in order to capture the correct information. This is difficult because there tends to be organic development of talent management and tracking systems

❖ the numbers of promotions from the talent pool.

The drivers behind talent management tracking include:

❖ improving the alignment of talent management techniques and strategies

* identifying potential senior executives much earlier in the talent process

* identifying high-performers or those with high potential in all parts of the organisation

* ensuring the appropriate quality and quantity of individuals on talent management programmes

* monitoring the rate of progression of employees on talent management programmes

* assessing performance against targets for internal or external recruits.

Whatever the prime reason for tracking, one of the lessons from evaluation of learning and development is that evaluation must be integrated into all stages of activities, rather than be thought about only post-activity. How much was this evident in the talent management research?

> Important aims for organisations in the evaluation of talent management are to understand which areas of talent management are strategic priorities, to identify the different but important elements, and to attempt to align these in a coherent framework.

One useful tool to achieve this is the balanced scorecard.

THE BALANCED SCORECARD AND ITS APPLICATION TO TALENT MANAGEMENT

The balanced scorecard originated as a method and a tool for the execution of an organisation's business strategy (Kaplan and Norton, 1996). The approach has now been drawn upon for functional strategies such as those in HR.

When applying this to talent management it may have the following functions:

* It highlights a selection of measures appropriate to the organisation's strategic circumstances.

* It can be used to create extensive and relevant data in the first instance, and then be used at regular intervals afterwards to monitor and evaluate progress and assist a new focus or identify new measures.

* It is also valuable in identifying relationships between different elements. For example, creative recruitment practices can enable organisational growth but clear expectations of performance management and appropriate development programmes will also be needed.

So how might this be reflected in practice? Figure 9, below, shows an example of what a talent management scorecard might look like for an organisation with strategic objectives of regenerating its product lines, organisational growth and improved customer relations.

Figure 9 ❖ An example of a talent management balanced scorecard

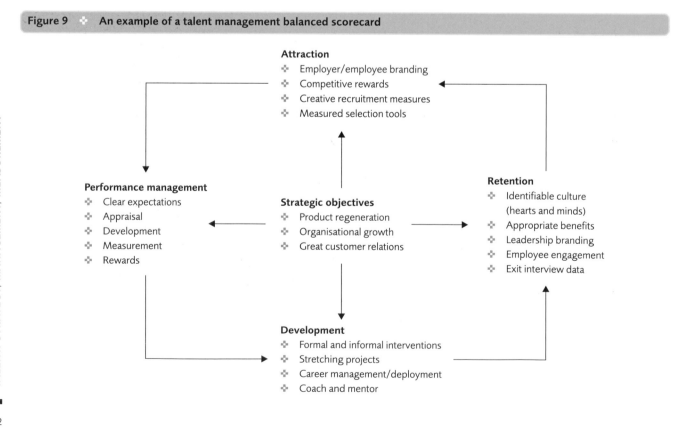

Attraction
* Employer/employee branding
* Competitive rewards
* Creative recruitment measures
* Measured selection tools

Performance management
* Clear expectations
* Appraisal
* Development
* Measurement
* Rewards

Strategic objectives
* Product regeneration
* Organisational growth
* Great customer relations

Retention
* Identifiable culture (hearts and minds)
* Appropriate benefits
* Leadership branding
* Employee engagement
* Exit interview data

Development
* Formal and informal interventions
* Stretching projects
* Career management/deployment
* Coach and mentor

Different organisations will have their own strategic objectives related to their own corporate environment and so will need to construct their own balanced scorecard populated with appropriate information or measures.

Standard Chartered PLC makes extensive use of the balanced scorecard approach. It has several clear and integrated scorecards showing the different elements of its strategic HR processes and how they are related. These are consolidated to produce a final human capital scorecard at year-end, and it is from this that external reporting information is developed.

As shown in Figure 10, below, talent management forms a key part of Standard Chartered PLC's roadmap and is integrated into other HR tracking activities. The underlying theme is that of organisational success through engaging organisational talent.

In Standard Chartered PLC human capital management involves a clear information and review process, including:

❖ a human resource information system that exports data into a series of bespoke spreadsheets quarterly and annually, and in different forms for particular parts of the business and countries

❖ a global report combing all the information, which comprises a series of slides with commentary to enable managers to understand the data

❖ twice-yearly board reviews on people strategy that form part of the annual strategy planning process

❖ a scorecard data review within each global business by a top team 'People Forum'

| Figure 10 ❖ Human capital measurement in Standard Chartered PLC |

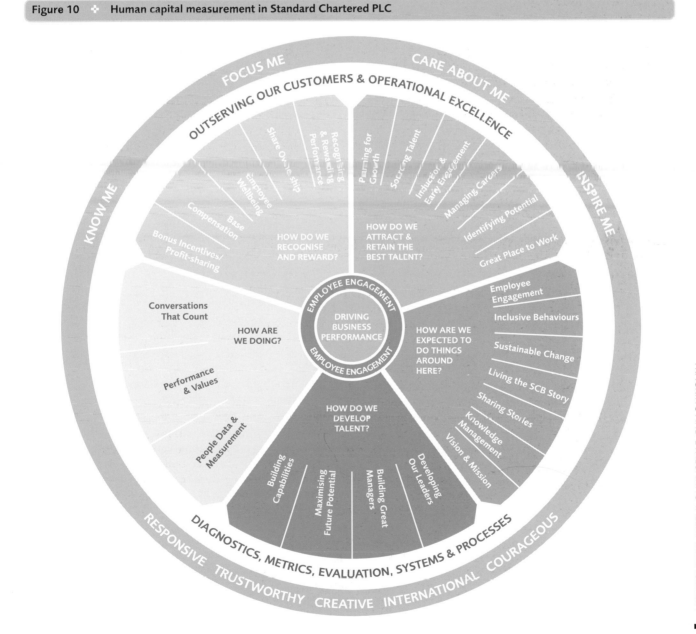

❖ at country level, local chief executive and management committee reviews of key trends in order to specify areas they ought to focus on.

Attrition, internal versus external recruitment, promotion rates, or whether people are achieving their personal development plans are all measured. However, Standard Chartered PLC also uses qualitative data to identify the role of the manager as mediating the relationship between engagement and performance. In turn, this has led to a focus on qualitative research to identify what raises the bank's best managers above the rest. A further example of the use of qualitative data is analysis of high performance in selected customer-facing roles to determine the key behaviours which continue to drive customer loyalty. These examples illustrate that measurement and metrics do not always have to be 'hard' numbers. This is important to bear in mind when evaluating talent management.

Standard Chartered PLC's metrics showed that the familiar measures – such as number of employees, turnover and information on pay and compensation – do not go far enough to align people management decisions with corporate objectives and to measure creation of shareholder value. Instead, Standard Chartered PLC is making efforts to create new sets of metrics. Their current metrics relate to those aspects which have traditionally been thought of as difficult to quantify – such as how engaged people are in their work and what entices them to leave the organisation – and which are of high relevance to talent management.

As reported in the second CIPD Human Capital Panel 2006 Report, Standard Chartered PLC has continued to evolve its external reporting through its Annual Review and its Sustainability Review, which release significantly more data than in the past, and the Bank is increasingly candid about the challenges it faces. In line with the Accounting for People Taskforce, there is a recognition that every organisation will have to determine how it intends to report externally. It is likely that ultimately a common core of metrics will be evident across each sector.

Some commentators have equated this process to the development and implementation of a 'talent supply chain'. This means applying the supply-chain business process to talent acquisition. In turn, this involves engaging with certain metrics that would not ordinarily be used, such as speed, cost, and efficiency of labour – ie labour as a commodity. It could involve activities such as a segmentation of those regarded as talented or identifying pivotal talent pools where the quality and/or availability of human capital makes the biggest difference to strategic success (Boudreau and Ramstad, 2005).

Tracking talent through the supply chain requires accurate reporting to identify where talented employees came from and how successfully they are being deployed. This would seem to be a basic requirement in any measurement activity.

One key evaluation question for organisations is 'How will we know when we are successful?'

> *What will define talent management in our organisation is when someone from our talent pool is Deputy Director of the organisation. That is when we will truly know that everything we have set out to achieve and the delivery mechanisms by which we have gone about developing talent have been successful.*

> Executive Director

For many organisations it will never be completely known when they have been successful because strategic boundaries move and the corporate environment is dynamic. This is a common experience for the HR function and development professionals. What matters is that there is a sound and logical basis, with reliable, relevant and accurate data, for making judgements about the value of talent management activities and any modifications that are needed.

OTHER MEASUREMENT CHALLENGES FOR TALENT MANAGEMENT

Our research identified a few more measurement challenges.

The first is that of measuring the progress of those identified as especially talented (although most of our case-study organisations took a broader view of talent, as noted in earlier chapters).

Gordon Ramsay's 'star performers' are examples of this. The HR director of Gordon Ramsay Holdings describes what training an employee – 'Jennifer' – might undertake in development courses to build her technical then managerial knowledge:

> *We train them. If 'Jennifer' is in the kitchen as a Commis-Chef or a Demi-chef or a Junior Sous, she would need to have a certain course, for example, for statutory food hygiene. If she goes for a more senior level ... which is no more than intermediate supervisory level, then [she would need] a management course within food hygiene. If it's a higher step that she takes ... we'll send her on a three-day course or maybe a five-day course to cover that. We often send them on a supervisory health and safety. [From] that aspect of things, they feel a lot more confident in managing a kitchen, they know what they are talking about, they can direct and lead.*

Keeping track of this type of talent is a priority for some organisations.

Another element of the talent pipeline where measurement is important is in relation to staff turnover – perhaps the most well-known but often inaccurately-used metric. A variety of well-known metrics are used by our case studies. Again, in Gordon Ramsay Holdings, their HR director told us:

> We have quite a high turnover if you look at the actual statistics. But as with everything, 70-75% of our staff stay with us for three years or longer: 25% of our staff turnover, many hundreds of percent a year for various reasons. We tend to be transient; we get a lot of students who want to work the summer. You've got to be a certain type of person to work in a Ramsay kitchen or a Ramsay restaurant, and a lot of people think, 'Yes, yes, I can do it' – and then they can't, so they leave.

The challenge for talent measurement therefore is to have accurate turnover statistics but to apply insights into the reasons behind these measures. (This is in fact a relevant conclusion to all aspects of talent measurement.)

The third area of talent measurement challenge was that of performance management. In Google, their European Director explained the process they used for salespeople:

> One of the guidelines we give all our salespeople when they join is that they should be spending two hours on the phone on a daily basis, and making approximately 40 calls a day. And we measure that and send a report out daily which shows them how they have performed for the previous day, so it shows them their talk-to-talk time . . . their number of calls, so they've got that information. We also measure them against the number of activations that they have – ie closed sales – and the revenue from those activations. Their bonus, their commission, is actually paid on the number of deals that they close in a quarter, and revenue not only from the deals that they close but deals that they have closed from previous sales as well, and the revenue stream carrying through as well, which is extremely important.

Some of these metrics can be characterised as input metrics and some as output metrics. It is the output metrics that are perceived to add value to the organisation.

Whether we are referring to talent tracking, the balanced scorecard or the supply chain for talent, technology is a valuable tool in the measurement process.

USING TECHNOLOGY IN TALENT TRACKING

There are a variety of forces that have impacted on the use of technology across HR during the past few years. As described in Parry *et al* (2006) these include the increase in self-service

applications, shared-service centres and the growing burden of employment legislation. Employers are looking for technology applications not only for operational HR functions but for more advanced functions too. And it is in this area where the advances in technology for HR measurement are likely to have most effect.

Employers are looking for the next-generation human capital management software. This software must take account of metrics for the whole talent management pipeline, and elements such as workforce management and workforce optimisation are critical areas. There also appears to be a desire to create innovative information databases on talent pools. This raises questions such as 'Is the software used for tracking fit for purpose and providing good access for all who need it?' and 'Who will be tracked, how closely, and how frequently?'

Few of the case studies have undertaken major investments on their human capital tools and technologies to ensure that as full a picture as possible is available on talent in their organisation. The NHS Trust is one example where plans exist to implement a relevant system. Where such systems do exist, one of the main drivers is the dynamic nature of the business environment and the need to respond to client requirements for particular skills, competences and talents.

This is likely to be an area of increasing importance for the talent management process in future.

IMPLICATIONS FOR PRACTICE

❖ *Talent tracking is a central part of the resource planning process* and individuals' progress through the elements of the talent pipeline is a helpful focus for both strategic planning and evaluation.

❖ *Developing a balanced scorecard* approach supports the tracking of talent and evaluation of talent management programmes.

❖ *Application of the talent supply chain* will support both talent tracking and talent management evaluation.

❖ *Relevant and appropriate metrics* are required to apply both balanced scorecard and human capital management techniques.

❖ *Both quantitative and qualitative data* must be collected and are of relevance and value.

❖ *Technology-based systems are significant enablers* of data collection, analysis, storage and presentation to stakeholders. Systems which support the tracking talent and evaluation of talent management are needed.

CONCLUSIONS AND PRACTICAL IMPLICATIONS

10

INTRODUCTION

The richness of the information from the case studies used in this report demonstrates a wide variety of possibilities when developing talent strategy and programmes. However, it is possible to draw some conclusions that can be used within those organisations who themselves are seeking to implement their own talent initiatives.

The research has shown that formal talent management is generally at an early stage of development, but there was evidence that it is increasingly being viewed as an important people management issue. The key driver moving it onto the corporate agenda is an immediate or predicted shortage of individuals with the required talents in the external labour market.

Talent management has proved to be a complex area to research because of the lack of a universal definition of talent or an established set of concepts and common language to refer to when talking about talent management.

The conclusions we have been able to draw are summarised below.

SOME IMPLICATIONS OF THE RESEARCH

Definitions and strategy

The experience of organisations, for example, shows that:

❖ What is seen as talent and how it is developed is highly organisation-specific. It depends on a combination of external and internal factors which vary according to the industry or sector, the nature of the work, the organisational culture, the approach to learning and development, as well as existing HR policies and practice. Notwithstanding that, there are some commonalities in the definitions of both talent and talent management.

❖ The characteristics most frequently associated with talented individuals are leadership behaviours, creativity, high levels of expertise and initiative. The significance attributed to these will depend on current organisational priorities.

❖ Changes in the external labour market, increased competition and skills shortages, recruitment and retention difficulties, a need to address the future leadership of the organisation and an acknowledged under-utilisation of the expertise of the existing workforce emerged as the main drivers for talent management in our case study organisations. These had different implications for every one of the case studies.

❖ The challenges stemming from their own organisational context was the key influence on their approach to attracting, developing and retaining talented individuals. The importance of employer branding in the pursuit of external talent is gaining increased recognition.

Given this complex background, organisations were grappling with developing a variety of approaches:

❖ There was a growing recognition of the value of an explicit strategy on how to attract, select, develop and manage the talents of individuals with high potential, but this was not universal. An informal ad hoc system for managing talent was the preferred option in some of our case organisations, particularly those constantly searching for the highest levels of expertise and creativity to maintain competitive advantage.

✤ For line managers there can be particular tensions in the application of talent management programmes. These arise from their wider managerial responsibilities for employees not in the identified talent pool as well as some challenges in terms of managing those who are. The main issue is one of the motivational impact on individuals who have not been selected for a talent initiative, particularly if developing a talent pool means reduced resources and less opportunity for progression for other employees. Those identified as talented can also feel uncomfortable in relation to their peers either because they have been formally singled out as talented or, equally, because they have been selected for a talent programme but it has not been made known.

✤ The HR specialist is regarded as a source of guidance and support across the range of provision that we encountered. Furthermore, the responsibility for developing talent management policies was largely perceived as falling in the domain of the HR function. Tying this in with the inclusion of HR in the corporate or business unit strategy setting process was seen as desirable, if not essential.

Having dealt with the process of definition and strategy, there were a variety of methods in executing talent management programmes.

Execution

✤ There are a number of choices to be made by organisations in selecting and managing its talent pool. There are issues of who is eligible, whether programmes are to be limited to certain occupational groups, the degree of transparent process, how individuals are to be selected, developed and tracked, as well as their progression and its equity in the light of existing equal opportunities policy and practice. This latter consideration is a particular concern to public sector employers who were found to be more inclined, despite budgetary constraints, to look at ways of widening employee access to talent management initiatives.

✤ The success of talent management activities are highly dependent on visible support from the very top of an organisation, namely at board level and from the CEO. The contributions of directors and senior managers are a critical factor in gaining the engagement of all the parties involved and the value they attach to any interventions. Once talent management activities are introduced, their success is heavily dependent on line managers. They have a pivotal role in identifying and nurturing talent, but they can also constrain talented individuals unless fully committed to talent management practices.

Then there was the whole question of how talent management is integrated within the wider HR or HRD domain.

Integration

✤ Where this has been thought through, it greatly enhances talent management initiatives. One such example is how an investment in developing coaching and mentoring provides a supportive organisational culture for talent management.

✤ Developing talent requires a blend of informal as well as formal learning interventions in order to 'stretch' participants on a talent management programme to broaden their experiential learning. A less structured approach can provide greater flexibility to accommodate different needs and supports the development of a more diverse talent pool.

✤ The future-focused nature of talent management can make it difficult to evaluate its real contribution mid-stream. Much of what is taking place is based on a belief in the importance of building up a pool of talent as a resource for the future benefit of the business. Organisational performance is viewed as the ultimate measure of success. It was evident from this study that organisational requirements for talent are dynamic and change over time, as will how success is measured.

✤ This makes it critical that there are mechanisms in place – such as a talent panel – which not only track what is happening to the talent pool but also review how talent management interventions are meeting organisational needs and adapt them as appropriate.

✤ Where organisations have successfully built up a pool of talent, the challenge senior managers face is how to deploy this resource to best advantage both for the organisation and to meet the aspirations of the individuals they have invested in.

KEY BENEFITS OF TALENT MANAGEMENT

The research revealed a number of potential benefits arising from talent management activities.

First, there is *the strategic contribution* made by talent management. It places organisational investment in human capital on the corporate agenda; requires a focus on HR planning (short-term and longer-term); and can contribute to other strategic objectives, such as the high-performance workplace, a learning organisation, being an employer of choice, and branding agenda and diversity management.

Second, effective talent management *has implications for resource management*. It creates a talent pool for future leadership and key organisational roles and provides a source of individuals to undertake special projects, change initiatives and secondments. It utilises and develops internal talent and reveals new talent not previously identified within an organisation. It can reduce recruitment costs as well as increase commitment and improve the retention of high-potential individuals. Finally, it focuses the investment in training and development.

Third, effective talent management *has a positive impact on other processes and practices*. It supports succession planning, for example. It can reinforce personal development planning in the performance review as well as promoting ownership of personal development. It encourages formal processes for tracking and monitoring individual progression.

Finally, the establishment of talent management can also *encourage new thinking*. It increases the potential for innovation and ideas from aspirational individuals for moving the organisation forward, as well as challenging the status quo. It offers a greater diversity of views and fresh perspectives on existing practice – for example, on job movement and mobility and on traditional career concepts.

KEY MESSAGES FOR TALENT MANAGEMENT PRACTICE

In summary, and based on research into a wide range of talent management practices, it is possible to ask the question whether there are any lessons that can be learned which have currency in most organisations. Are there some common factors that can transcend the specifics of any one organisation? The research suggests that there are ten key messages – which are outlined in the box overleaf:

TEN KEY MESSAGES

1 The starting point in the development of a talent management strategy or a talent management intervention, is to identify *how the organisation defines talent.*

2 Equally important is communicating *what is seen as talent and developing a language for talent management activities* that is understood by all the parties in the employment relationship.

3 *Support for talent management must flow from those at the very top of an organisation.* The value of their visible support for talent management initiatives is pivotal to how these are regarded and valued. A talent panel is a particularly useful means of ensuring the involvement of directors and senior management, especially when it has representation from across the organisation.

4 *Talent management activities should be developed with other HR policies and practice.* For example, its relationship with succession planning or diversity initiatives must be carefully thought through. To work effectively, these must be joined up. This will minimise the tensions they can create for busy line managers and provide clarity for employees about organisational priorities.

5 *HR specialists have an important role to play in providing support and guidance in the design and development of approaches to talent management that will fit the needs of the organisation.* To do this it is vital that they have a proper understanding of the challenges facing the organisation in attracting, recruiting, developing and retaining talented people to meet its immediate and future resourcing requirements. They must also have the knowledge to advise the organisation of alternative approaches to meeting its needs. This means that HR or talent management specialists must explore talent management practices in other industries to be able to advise on the best fit for their own organisation.

6 *Engaging line managers from an early stage is critical to ensure that they are committed to organisational approaches to talent management.* Their involvement in developing initiatives as well as identifying talent and nurturing talent is a priority area for attention in the implementation of any talent management activities.

7 *Talent management can be used to enhance an organisation's image: it supports employer branding in the labour market and provides a means of enhancing employee engagement to improve retention.* It can also be a means of maximising internal employee potential, which may be an even more effective way of gaining employee commitment.

8 *A proactive, strategic approach to talent management offers considerable organisational benefits in terms of developing a pool of talent as a resource to meet identified needs.* This should be complemented by a planned approach to utilising and progressing individuals who have participated in talent management programmes. They will have built up expectations. If their talents are not put to proper use, the risk is that they will lose commitment to the organisation and, having been developed, have an increased attraction to another employer.

9 *Developing talent relies on a blend of informal and formal methods.* The mix will depend on the needs of individuals on a particular programme, but a planned investment in developing coaches and mentors throughout an organisation pays dividends in providing a supportive culture for talent management. This will be enhanced in organisations where personal development planning is a core element of a performance review process.

10 *Processes must be developed to track the performance and progress of those identified in the talent pool* as well as systems for reviewing, refining and making changes to talent management initiatives to reflect changing organisational priorities.

REFERENCES

ARMSTRONG, M. and BARON, A. (2005)

Managing Performance: Performance management in action. London: CIPD

BARON, A. and ARMSTRONG, M. (2007)

Human Capital Management – Achieving Value through People. London: Kogan Page

BONNEY, N. (2005)

Overworked Britons? Part-time work and work–life balance, *Work, Employment and Society,* Vol 19, No 2: 391–401

BOUDREAU, J. W. and RAMSTAD, P. M. (2005)

Talentship, talent segmentation, and sustainability: a new HR decision science paradigm for a new strategy definition, *Human Resource Management,* Vol.44, Issue 2, Summer: 129–36

CANNON, J. and MCGEE, R. (2007)

Talent Management and Succession Planning. London: CIPD

CHARTERED INSTITUTE OF PERSONNEL AND DEVELOPMENT (2004)

Women in the Boardroom: A bird's eye view. Change Agenda. London: CIPD. Available at http://www.cipd.co.uk/onlineinfodocuments [Accessed 16 March 2007]

CHARTERED INSTITUTE OF PERSONNEL AND DEVELOPMENT (2005)

Learning and Development 2005. Survey report. London: CIPD. Available at http://www.cipd.co.uk/onlineinfodocuments [Accessed 16 March 2007]

CHARTERED INSTITUTE OF PERSONNEL AND DEVELOPMENT (2006)

Coaching Supervision. A paper prepared for the CIPD Coaching conference by Dr Peter Hawkins and Gil Schwenk

CHARTERED INSTITUTE OF PERSONNEL AND DEVELOPMENT (2006)

Learning and Development 2006. Survey report. London: CIPD. Available at http://www.cipd.co.uk/onlineinfodocuments [Accessed 16 March 2007]

CHARTERED INSTITUTE OF PERSONNEL AND DEVELOPMENT (2006)

Reflections on Talent Management. Change Agenda. London: CIPD. Available at http://www.cipd.co.uk/onlineinfodocuments

CHARTERED INSTITUTE OF PERSONNEL AND DEVELOPMENT (2006)

Talent Management: Understanding the dimensions. Change Agenda. London: CIPD. Available at http://www.cipd.co.uk/onlineinfodocuments [Accessed 16 March 2007]

CHARTERED INSTITUTE OF PERSONNEL AND DEVELOPMENT (2006)

Recruitment, Retention and Turnover 2006. Survey report. London: CIPD. Available at http://www.cipd.co.uk/onlineinfodocuments [Accessed 16 March 2007]

CHARTERED INSTITUTE OF PERSONNEL AND DEVELOPMENT (2006)

Human Capital Evaluation: Getting started. Human Capital Panel Report. London: CIPD. Available at http://www.cipd.co.uk/onlineinfodocuments [Accessed 16 March 2007]

CHARTERED INSTITUTE OF PERSONNEL AND DEVELOPMENT (2006)

Human Capital Evaluation: Evolving the data. Human Capital Panel Report. London: CIPD. Available at http://www.cipd.co.uk/onlineinfodocuments [Accessed 16 March 2007]

CHARTERED INSTITUTE OF PERSONNEL AND DEVELOPMENT (2006)

HR and Technology: Beyond delivery. Change Agenda. London: CIPD. Available at http://www.cipd.co.uk/onlineinfodocuments [Accessed 16 March 2007]

CHARTERED MANAGEMENT INSTITUTE (2006)

Measures of Workforce Capability for Future Performance. London: Chartered Management Institute

EDWARDS, M. (2005)

Employer and employee branding: HR or PR? In: Bach, S. (ed) *Managing Human Resources.*, 4th edition. Oxford: Blackwell: 266–86

EOC (2005)

Britain's Hidden Brain Drain: Final report. London: Equal Opportunities Commission

GIAMBATISTA, R. C., ROWE, R. G and RIAZ, S. (2005)

Nothing succeeds like succession: a critical review of leader succession literature since 1994, *The Leadership Quarterly*, Vol.16, No.6: 963–91

GRANT, L., YEANDE, S. and BUCHENER, L. (2005)

Working Below Potential: Women and part-time work. London: Equal Opportunities Commission

HIGGS, D. (2003)

Review of the role and effectiveness of non-executive directors. January. London: Department of Trade and Industry

HIRSH, W. (2000)

Succession Planning Demystified. Brighton: Institute for Employment Studies

HUTCHINSON, S. and PURCELL, J. (2003)

Bringing Policies to Life: The vital role of front line managers in people management. Executive Briefing. London: CIPD

HUTCHINSON, S. and PURCELL, J. (2007)

Learning and Development and the Line Manager. Change Agenda. London: CIPD

INNECTO REWARD CONSULTING (2006)

High flyer trend report. Available at: http://www.innectogroup.co.uk [Accessed 16 March 2007]

KAPLAN, R. S. and NORTON, D. P. (1996)

The Balanced Scorecard: Translating strategy into action. Boston, MA: Harvard Business School Press

KERSLEY, B., CARMEN, A., FORTH, J., BRYSON, A., BEWLEY, A., DIX, G. and OXENBRIDGE, S. (2006)

Inside the Workplace - First Findings from the 2004 Workplace Employment Relations Survey. Available from WERS 2004, URL:http://www.dti.gov.uk/er/inside

MARDJONO, A. (2005)

A tale of corporate governance: lessons why firms fail, *Managerial Auditing Journal*, Vol.20, No.3: 272–83.

MARTIN, G. and HETRICK, S. (2006)

Corporate Reputations, Branding and People Management. Oxford: Butterworth-Heinemann

MATTHEWMAN, J. and MATIGNON, F. (2005)

Human Capital Reporting: An internal perspective. A guide. London: CIPD

O'NEIL, D. A. and BILIMORIA, D. (2005)

Women's career development phases: idealism, endurance, and reinvention, *Career Development International*, Vol.10, No.3: 168–89

PARRY, E., TYSON, S., SELBIE, D. and LEIGHTON, R. (2006)

HR and technology: impact and advantages. Research Report. London: CIPD

RAYMAN-BACCHUS, L. (2003)

Contextualising corporate governance, *Managerial Auditing Journal*, Vol.18, No.3: 180–92

RUBIN, J. P. (2006)

The CEO's Role in Talent Management: How top executives from ten countries are nurturing the leaders of tomorrow. London: DDI/Economist Intelligence Unit

SCARBROUGH, H. and ELIAS, J. (2002)

Evaluating Human Capital. London: CIPD

SOCPO (2005)

Talent Management – The capacity to make a difference. London: The Society for Chief Personnel Officers/Veredus

SYEDAIN, H. (2007)

A Talent for Numbers, *People Management*, Vol.13, No.12, 14 June: 36

TOWERS PERRIN (2004)

Reconnecting with Employees: Attracting, engaging and retaining your workforce: 2004 European Talent Survey. London: Towers Perrin

TRUSS, K., SOANE, E. and EDWARDS, C. (2006)

Working Life: Employee attitudes and engagement 2006. London: CIPD

ULRICH, D. (1997)

Human Resource Champions. Boston, MA: Harvard University Press

VERHAAR, C. H. and SMULDERS, H. R. (1999)

Employability in Practice, *Journal of European Industrial Training*, Vol.23, No.6: 268–74

VISE, D. (2005)

The Google Story. London: Macmillan

WARREN, C. (2006)

Talent management curtain call, *People Management*, Vol.12, No.6, 23 March: 24–9

WILLOCK, R. (2005)

Employer branding is key in fight for talent, *Personnel Today*, 17 May: 4